Table of Contents

1- Introduction
2- Time – Most Valuable Asset
3- Who Can Bag A Millionaire
4- Types Of Rich
5- Keep It To Yourself
6- Your Mind
7- Rich Mindset
8- Create Vision Boards
9- Your Circle
10- Move Where The Affluent People Live
11- Your Income
12- What Age And Size You Have To Be
13- Hair
14- Eyebrows
15- Eyes & Eyelashes
16- Lips
17- Teeth
18- Skin
19- Acne
20- Nails
21- Rich Men & Fake – Looking Women
22- Never Have Affairs With Married Men
23- Study Your Body
24- Body Shapes
25- Colours
26- Materials
27- Clothes
28- Underwear
29- Tops, Blouses, Shirts
30- Trousers & Jeans
31- Skirts
32- Dresses
33- Blazers & Jackets
34- Coats
35- Accessories
36- Footwear

37- Bags
38- Capsule Wardrobe
39- Choosing Your Perfume
40- Dress Codes
41- Posture And Deportment
42- Manners
43- Learn To Be Elegant
44- Role Models
45- Mentors
46- Your Home
47- Networking
48- Annual Events
49- Where Do The Rich Go On Holiday
50- Food
51- Drinks
52- How To Hold The Wine & Champagne Glass
53- Smoking
54- How To Converse
55- Facial Expression
56- What You Read
57- Who Pays The Bill
58- Thank You Notes
59- Where Do You Find Rich Men
60- How To Move To An Affluent Area For Less
61- Skills To Learn
62- Your Social Media
63- First Date
64- The Unnecessary Games
65- And Then, What?
66- Be Kind!
67- Believe

INTRODUCTION

After studying many wealthy individuals for more than two decades, I decided to write this book, as understanding the mindset of a rich man may make it easier for the reader to determine if they would like to be in a relationship with one.

I didn't write the book to make women feel good or bad about themselves. My intention was not to "empower" women of all sizes and habits. Instead, I wrote the book for women ready to acknowledge bad manners, poor habits, toxic people and environments, and who wish to start doing something to change them. So, if you get easily offended, do not read this book!

In the following chapters, you may find things which could upset you, especially when you read about certain physical appearance aspects that rich men do not like in a woman. Those things may seem mean or unfair. However, it is essential to understand that what I relay here are the likes and dislikes of wealthy individuals regarding what THEY find beautiful.

If you don't fit their criteria but are happy and flourishing as you are, you have already won the game of life and don't need to concern yourself with what rich men prefer. Be however you wish!

This book is for women who want to elevate themselves, change their social circle and ultimately meet and date a wealthy man. Therefore, the advice given here may not be for you but may be helpful to someone else.

~ 2 ~

TIME:
THE MOST VALUABLE ASSET

Like everyone else, rich people have likes and dislikes. Some care about their looks and others don't; some have excellent manners, others don't; some have vices, others have high morals, some are generous, and some are not.

But what ALL wealthy people seem to have in common (that people who are not wealthy don't always have) is a recognition of worth for their time. Individuals with considerable wealth value their time immensely, as they understand that lost time is something they cannot reclaim. They can lose money, and they may make it back. They can lose material things and repurchase them. But they know they can never recover lost time. And although time reduces for everyone - rich or poor - the rich are much more aware of the importance of lost time.

Rich people are busy, and because they meet many new people, they must learn to select fast when it comes to timewasters. So, if they feel that someone doesn't bring any value to their lives, they don't stick around.

Time is precious to them, both in business and personal lives. So, when it comes to women, as in business and friendships, they decide within seconds of meeting a woman . if she sparks any interest.

Good men will always appreciate all the qualities in a woman. But they don't necessarily become intrigued and develop a desire to know more about a woman if she is not exceptional in every way.

Men with lower income can be more patient and give a chance to an attractive woman who behaved questionably on a first encounter. They may put it down to the fact that she may have been nervous, misguided, in a lousy mood, etc., and they may decide to allow more time to get to know the woman.

Rich people don't do this. They allocate only a certain amount of time to meeting a woman. If she didn't make an excellent first impression, she lost her chance for a second date. Rich men don't allow additional time for a person to repair a first impression which has gone the wrong way. They treasure their time and use it wisely.

If this is all you take from this book, memorise it and remember it forever: if you have the chance to meet a wealthy individual, in business or personal life, show your best self; otherwise, you may miss out on the opportunity to form a connection with that person.

If a classy gentleman meets an attractive woman, but she is loud, obnoxious, wears too much makeup, has a lot of plastic surgeries, flashes too much flesh, etc., I can assure you that he will not be intrigued.

In their world, classy gentlemen see many beautiful, decent, feminine, natural, and elegant women. So, they don't need to waste their time with someone who didn't make a great first impression.

Rich people get rich because of the choices they make. And because successful men are high achievers, they want to win in business **and** when choosing their spouses. To a rich man, an attractive woman possesses natural beauty, elegance, intelligence, and class.

Please note that I am talking here about a specific type of wealthy man: the classy type. Some less refined men are excited when a lot of flesh is on show, so it's entirely up to you what calibre of people you would like to meet.

~ 3 ~

WHO CAN "BAG" A MILLIONAIRE?

• Any woman who comes from a wealthy background
• Any woman who is a self-made millionaire
• Any woman who is with a man who is working towards becoming a millionaire
• Any woman who is lucky enough to meet a millionaire who will take a shine to her

• And any woman who follows a well-designed action plan

If you don't come from a wealthy background, are not a self-made millionaire, are not in a relationship with a driven partner (who is working towards becoming wealthy), or don't feel lucky, YOU MUST EXECUTE THE PLAN!

Also, although most affluent men like beautiful, intelligent, classy women, not every rich person you will meet will necessarily have the best manners, dress well, or be the most refined. So, it's up to you to decide what type of rich man you want to meet.

~ 4 ~

TYPES OF RICH

There are different types of rich, and here are the three main categories:

1) OLD MONEY - wealthy people who maintained their wealth over many generations

You will find Old Money as board members of various foundations and charities; they have high ranks in the army, some are politicians or diplomats, or may have top positions in finance and law.

Some own large organisations and art galleries; some are museum directors or may be affiliated with culture and entertainment. The Old Money men often own considerable land and real estate.

The rich in this category own heirlooms, and often, their places are old and outdated. They are highly educated, have impeccable manners and do not like showing off their wealth. Sometimes they may even come across as stingy. They are familiar with all the social events and know how to behave in any social situation. They like beautiful women and may have flings with women from a different class, but they are likely to choose from the same category when they marry. Even if, sometimes, the woman may not possess what some may call "a classic beauty". However, being from a similar background, she will be familiar with the rich world and wouldn't need any training in etiquette and civility.

The men in this category often ought to please the family when choosing a spouse, as they must continue the tradition of merging two affluent clans. Some men in this category may fall in love with a woman of modest background and have a great relationship, but they will be very pragmatic and choose someone more "suitable" for marriage.

However, there are cases where Old Money marries someone from a modest background if she is well-educated and has excellent manners.

2) NEW MONEY (MODEST BACKGROUND) - self-made millionaires who weren't born into wealth

New Money from a modest background made their wealth by taking chances or being great sellers or professionals who started from nothing and climbed the professional ladder. They are successful entrepreneurs, in various industries, from restaurants to retail, to real estate, to banking, to technology, media and communications sector, and they often invest in start-ups.

Their places are very new and high-tech, they are big spenders, and SOME men in this category are not necessarily highly educated or well-mannered.

Some may not be familiar with all the elite events, and in some cases, their manners are basic. Many feel the need to splash the cash. They show off their wealth and speak openly about money, multimillion-dollar deals, and high prices. They are very generous, and the physical aspect is essential when they look for a partner.

Unlike Old Money, when men in this category fall in love, they don't usually care about the woman's background but prefer their spouse to be good-looking, feminine, intelligent, and kind.

Very rarely will you see a man in this category marry a plain-looking woman; most of the time, their spouses are stunning.

3) NEW MONEY (WELL-OFF BACKGROUND) - millionaires who are privately educated and come from the middle class and upper middle class, but they increased their wealth considerably, making them part of the "New Money" category

They have professional parents and a good education. They made their Money in

Investment Banking, Hedge Fund, top medical professions, corporate law, diplomacy, politics, technology, media and communications, real estate, energy etc.

The men in this category understand the social calendar and the protocol, are usually very generous, and appreciate women's beauty. They are also more discreet about their wealth. **This type is the type of millionaire you will meet the most.**

Just like the men in the previous two categories, they prefer beauty, intelligence, and refinement when choosing spouses. And although they come from the middle or upper middle class, they don't necessarily care if their partner is from a similar background.

However, they care about their spouse's demeanour because the social life is important to them. So, even if the woman is not always strikingly beautiful, she is undoubtedly very classy.

Although rich men fit mainly in the above three groups with their respective characteristics, it doesn't mean everyone born with money is well-mannered but stingy. The same as not everyone who is a self-made millionaire is generous but lacks social skills.

It is a generalisation, and there are exceptions.

For example, you will meet many very generous aristocrats, just as you will meet many self-made millionaires with impeccable manners.

It doesn't matter to which social class the man belongs; if you present yourself in an elevated manner, everyone will appreciate and admire you: Old Money or New Money!

The aristocrat will respect and welcome you because elegance and class surround his world.

The self-made millionaire will admire and respect you because he is a high achiever and likes to be a winner in love (just like in business), so he sets his standards extremely high.

It's important to remember that:
- Even if you notice errors in the way others conduct themselves (outside of your close circle of friends and family), you should never point out the mistakes or humiliate

anyone! Elegance is the ability to make others feel good around you.

\- You must distance yourself from anyone who doesn't respect you; it doesn't matter how much money they may have. You should never compromise, and you should never stay in toxic relationships or environments.

There are many incredible men out there! Find one who respects and loves you and whom you respect and love!

***

As an afterthought, I would like to mention a new category of the rich who made money from YouTube, music, cryptocurrency, etc. And the men in this last category can be very different: from someone like Mark Zuckerberg - very private and modest, to someone like Kanye West – who prefers a different kind of woman. But, for obvious reasons, I will leave this category out.

I will focus on the three categories mentioned above:
- Old Money
- New Money (modest background)
- New Money (well-off background)

~ 5 ~

KEEP IT TO YOURSELF

You may be reading this book:
- for pure amusement
- because you ran out of things to be outraged about
- because you want to learn tips on elevating yourself
- because you want to meet (and perhaps date) wealthy individuals

I will not elaborate on the first three reasons.
If you amused yourself, got outraged, or learned a few tips on becoming more refined, then it's OK!

However, if the real reason for purchasing this book is a desire to follow the plan step by step, elevate yourself, and meet wealthy people (hopefully, the man of your dreams, too), then the first thing you should do is: **keep your intentions (and this project) to yourself!**

If you talk to friends and family about your intentions, it is doubtful that everyone would support the idea. And that's OK!

It's only human for people to have pessimistic views about something they don't understand or don't see themselves doing. That, however, doesn't mean you should allow their opinions to affect your decisions.

The less you care about things that DON'T matter, and the more you care about things that DO matter, the happier you will feel.

If you don't purposely hurt anyone, people's opinions should not concern you. So, accepting that you cannot control people's minds will set you free. Their minds - their battles! Never fight other people's battles. Instead, fight YOURS because you may stand a chance of winning.

Keeping this to yourself doesn't necessarily mean you lie to your friends and family. It is merely your decision to keep quiet about a project which will take time, effort, and dedication. You will not want to have other people's opinions influencing your flow.

If you can't keep the project to yourself and want to talk to your friends and family about it, you can do so, but be aware that not everyone will be supportive.

As a general piece of advice: when someone is against your idea, thoroughly study the person. Is the person at peace with their health, career, finance, and love? Because if that person is not satisfied with every aspect of their life, they shouldn't advise others.

People can only advise from their perspective.
And if they haven't tried completing this project, if they are not part of a circle of wealthy individuals, or if they didn't go out with a millionaire before, their view would be of someone who didn't experience the same things you are seeking to achieve.

How would they know, then? Why would they decide that your goal to have a more elevated life is terrible if they haven't tried it?

If an unsuccessful individual says they wouldn't want to have Bill Gates' money, don't believe them! Because they wouldn't know how it feels to have Bill Gates' money. Only when you've experienced how it feels to be that rich can you form an opinion about it. Otherwise, it's just an assumption.

So, if it's not harmful, illegal, or immoral, never listen to someone who tells you that you shouldn't do something if they've never experienced that something.

If you want to enjoy the finer things in life, you shouldn't worry about someone who hasn't had the experience. Their opinion shouldn't influence your decisions. Instead, tell them that you understand it's not something they would do, but you would like to give it a go.

And if you decide that this project is not for you and want to give up halfway, at least you've learned some tips on becoming more refined. And even for this reason alone, it would be worth reading the book.

But if you choose to go ahead and pull through the tough times, you will end up with a network of exciting and successful connections, and you may also get to meet a great guy. The changes in your life will be significant, and you will feel it was all worth it.

And yes, before you succeed, there will be some tough times:
- Sometimes you will feel like you want to give up because it's too complicated.

- There will be times when you meet people who will disappoint you.
- Other times, you will feel like you can't "fake it till you make it" any longer.
- You will also have days when you may find the whole process tiring and too much work.
- There will be times when you will feel very lonely.

Be prepared, because it may be a long and arduous journey, and you will need the grit to overcome any unpleasantries you may encounter along the way.

If it were easy, everyone would do it. But it can be challenging, which is why less people overcome their backgrounds and do more in life. Most of the people live mediocre lives.

And yes, you may meet some wealthy individuals who are not necessarily pleasant, but you will learn how to filter the bad ones.

You probably already know many unsuccessful and unprosperous people who are not pleasant. Therefore, even if you are not interested in meeting someone wealthy, you always go through recognising and disposing of the wrong people in your life.

There are good and bad people among the wealthy and good and bad people among the non-wealthy.

Identifying and selecting the good guys from the bad guys is the same in any social class.

If you are exposed to people who are not particularly successful, you use your common sense to select good people from bad people.
If you are exposed to successful people, you use the same common sense to select good people from bad people.

It takes the same effort to select good people from either lot. So, make sure you know enough successful and wealthy people to be able to choose nice individuals from the wealthy lot, instead of being forced to choose nice individuals from the unsuccessful lot. This way, you will surround yourself with kind, friendly people who can also inspire you with their success.

You must remember that friendly people who live mediocre lives are not always inspiring. So, be around individuals who can help you grow.

While doing this project, being aware that you might come across duplicitous and hypocritical people will help you to not get disheartened by the few bad ones you will meet along the way. I can assure you that there are some fantastic people out there!

And you must also know that, before you build your network and figure out everyone you meet (to be able to keep a bunch of genuine friends and acquaintances), there will be times when you will feel lonely and perhaps alienated from your old friends. But it's only a temporary feeling.

Spending time with yourself is, sometimes, a blessing.
By loving your company, cherishing memories of the past and dreams of the future and enjoying every moment (even the moments spent alone), you will experience contentment and bliss.

And contentment and bliss will help you carry on and reach your goals. So, have a break when you feel tired and overwhelmed, but don't give up! This project will change your life if you do it step by step and with utmost care.

You must feel that you want this WITH EVERY FIBRE OF YOUR BEING! If failing, go back to the drawing board and start again! Never stop trying if you have setbacks!

Follow each step religiously, read and re-read carefully, and trust the process!
The plan only works for people who are determined to fulfil their dreams.
The plan only works for people who follow it step by step.

TO SUM UP:
- Decide to embark on this journey
- Ideally, don't tell people
- If you do tell people, expect criticism
- Develop a thick skin but be polite about other people's views
- Pay attention to the new people you meet
- Filter out the bad acquaintances
- Surround yourself with inspiring people
- Continue to do the project, even when it gets tough and when you may feel lonely
- Follow the plan, step by step, without rushing the process
- Learn to love the time you spend with yourself
- Cherish the new YOU

YOUR MIND

"To be able to shape your future, you have to be willing and able to change your paradigm" - Joel Barker (Paradigms: The Business of Discovering the Future)

Most of us carry emotional baggage, which can create blockages. And we must clear these blockages to allow progress. But unfortunately, in many cases, people are unaware of the hindrance that stops their growth.

Different people may carry blockages from various situations:

1) You may feel you lack self-esteem and seem to repeat a pattern: you get into relationships with men who don't treat you right because you don't hold yourself in high regard. If it happens often enough, you may start seeing the pattern, but you need help understanding the root of your problem. For example, the lack of self-esteem may have resulted from something in the past, and now it obstructs your energy flow. And this needs to be cleared.

2) You may feel that in every job you have ever had, you progress up to a point, and then you stagnate without being able to climb the professional ladder to a higher level, even though you work hard. You see the pattern but tell yourself that this is all you can do or blame it on the circumstances. This is a blockage, and you sabotage your progress by believing (on a subconscious level) that you don't deserve the promotion or career growth.

3) You don't like some of your friends but still waste much of your time with them. You complain about one to the other, yet you still see them regularly.

And it's always the same: after meeting them, you leave feeling annoyed and displeased with something done or said. You know you don't like those friends, but you can't say no to them. The same thing may happen with some family members too.

What pushes you to such toxic environments could be emotions you repressed for too long because they were too hard to address and resolve.

Perhaps, in the past, an event or a situation made you look like a bad person. You lived the feeling of guilt with such intensity that you are now afraid to look again like a bad person if you refuse something.

But you must start saying no to people! Don't be a pushover any longer!

4) You know you've put on weight, but every time you start a healthy diet, you give up after a few days because it's easier to grab something unhealthy than cook something healthy.

5) You have money problems but still spend on clothes you'll never wear and things you'll never use.

You do some or all of the above continuously and get depressed when you see other people's lives and successes.

It may even cross your mind that you must make different choices to have a different experience, but staying in your comfort zone is easier. So, another month passes, and then another year passes, and you look at your life, and there is little change or growth from one year to the next.

You shouldn't be surprised if your life stays the same. It is YOUR choice!

We were born to grow and flourish. And if you are not doing it, if there is no progress with every passing year, something happened somewhere in your past that stomped your growth. So, you need to unblock that something to grow and flourish.

It's terrifying to think that you go through life without progressing. Stagnating is unhealthy. Progress is healthy.

Your subconscious mind is fascinating and compelling and it can be your enemy or friend. It can remember things that happened in your childhood, which can stop you from progressing, and even fabricate things that never happened!

When you were little, the boy who pushed you in the playground may have ignited a strong feeling which stayed inside you, making you feel frustrated and helpless.

When you are awake, you may not even remember the episode, but in a hypnotic state, your mind can take you there, reliving the frustration and the feeling of helplessness. If you don't deal with it, frustration and helplessness will appear at the most pivotal moments. And those feelings of frustration and powerlessness will become obstacles to your growth.

Specialists agree that during sessions of hypnosis, some people relive things from their childhood with such intensity, only to realise (when they were awake) that some of the events never occurred. Family and relatives were able to confirm they never happened. Maybe they were dreams or things from films watched during their childhood; no one could tell. But they felt these made-up events with such intensity that their subconscious mind created blockages which stayed with them, carrying the consequences into their adult lives.

Of course, not all the things experienced under hypnosis are figments of imagination.

Most things people relive in a hypnotic state are actual past events, but this is an example of how your mind can deceive and sabotage your life. An unhealthy mind needs healing.

Without studying ourselves, we don't know how much baggage we carry in this journey called "life". We don't know how harmful some of the "baggage" is, and we lug our heavy baggage for far too long before deciding to seek help and let go of it.

Healing the mind is one of the most extraordinary acts of self-love. The inner peace you feel when you calm and silence a troubled mind is beautiful. And when you start experiencing that state of beauty, you cannot go back to allowing others to enter your sacred place (your mind) with ill intentions.

When you heal, you will outgrow friends and will no longer want to be in toxic environments where people moan and complain about everything. You will feel enlightened when you learn to enjoy a state of equilibrium and peace.

Spend time anywhere in nature, even in a little garden or a local park. Connecting with nature can boost the immune system, reduce stress, and increase energy levels. It can even heal and help with recovering from illnesses. So, spend time in nature without your phone and any other distractions.

To heal, some people choose therapy, some choose hypnosis, and others prefer to meditate, breathe, and sit in silence.
Do what feels right for you, and don't give up until you heal your mind and clear your blockages!

Ideally would be for you to use all the following methods simultaneously:
- listen to binaural beats and sounds of a specific frequency for mind healing
- listen to mantras for abundance and wellbeing
- record your voice for 10 - 20 minutes with the same message, to which you should listen daily
- practice guided meditation
- repeat affirmations
- practice self-hypnosis
- have some sessions with a hypnotherapist, psychotherapist, or psychiatrist (if needed)
- read books about changing your mindset
- listen to audiobooks about success
- keep crystals at home and carry some with you
- create vision boards with your goals and dreams
- connect with nature

Changing your mindset requires discipline, which must become a lifestyle, not something you only do temporarily. Create a routine, introduce all the above points into your daily activities, and follow that routine.

If you travel in the depths of your mind, you have the power to be anything you want. You can close your eyes right now, be anything you want and live your desired life.

Do that every day! It doesn't require effort and is incredibly beneficial for your mental state.

You don't need to study intensely to meditate to know how to do it correctly. Instead, close your eyes, take deep breaths to relax and imagine living the life you want. This way, you are giving your mind a break so that it can heal. Being able to live your desired life in your mind is a blessing. So, enjoy the feeling, be grateful, and do it often. Make it your unique oasis of tranquillity, where you go to seek refuge from reality.

Don't worry about anyone who tells you that these things are silly! People who dismiss things that can only benefit your mental health are unhappy with their lives.

How do you know when your mind heals?
- When you start believing everything is possible
- When your mind is so uncluttered that you feel the same way that you felt when you were a child and believed you were invincible
- When your dreams are colossal, and you don't find them silly

- When you will stop blaming people and situations and instead start looking for opportunities

When you feel all these, your mind has healed, and you can start your journey.

Now, you can plant your seeds in well-nourished soil and begin enjoying the fruits of your labour. Your seeds are your dreams.

When your mind is healed and open to changes, you will notice a transformation and not want to return to a previous state.

You will outgrow some people in your life.

You will begin to admire other people's successes and not feel envy. You will want to surround yourself with healthy, happy, and prosperous people to become the same.

You will start seeing more abundance around you (in nature, places, and people) and crave your oasis of tranquillity, where you quiet your mind, meditate and allow your dreams to take shape.

For now, you can call this oasis your "imaginary world".

But if you "feel" the "imaginary world" with all your senses and IF YOU START

MAKING CHANGES IN YOUR HABITS, your imaginary world will become your real world.

Your health, job, body, financial situation, and friends are products of your choices.

No one forces you to be moody and envious.
No one forces you to stay in an unwanted job and not look for something else.
No one forces you to eat all the bad things you eat.
No one forces you to spend money on things you don't need.
No one forces you to befriend people you don't like.

You have the freedom to set yourself free from all harmful things.

If your diet is unhealthy, it's your choice.
If you go to a job you don't like every day, it's your choice.
If your relationships are toxic, it's your choice.
If you are unhappy, it's your choice.
Everything in your life is your choice.

And yes, changes are sometimes inconvenient and painful, but you can start (with small steps) building different habits.

Developing a bad habit is no different from developing a good one, so start creating new good habits or replace the bad ones:

Do you like crisps?
Change the potato crisps to seaweed and vegetable crisps. If you don't have potato crisps in the house and seaweed and vegetable crisps are the only options for a savoury snack, you will eat the ones you have. These options are not only healthy, but they are also tasty. So, start replacing bad snacks with good snacks!

Do you like your daily glass of wine?
Keep kombucha in the house and have a glass of that instead. It's tingly on the tongue, and it tastes a little sour. Yes, it will not have the same effect as wine, but you must learn to replace bad habits with good habits. Serve the kombucha in a wine glass and sip it slowly, as you would do with wine. You will start enjoying it. But remember that kombucha is a fermented tea with some caffeine, so find a substitute (such as lemon water or a sugarless drink) if you want to have it late in the evening.

Do you like sweets?
Have a few grapes or some berries instead. If you don't buy sweets to keep in the house,

when you fancy something sweet, grapes or berries will do.

You don't exercise enough because you don't like going to the gym?
Find a few songs you love and dance to them. Dance intensely to give your body a good workout. And walk as much as you can and as often as you can. Walking is therapeutic and burns calories.

Do you feel that you spend too much time with uninspiring friends?
Sometimes, decline their invitation and tell them you want to spend time with yourself. You don't need to give many explanations to people. If you don't purposely hurt someone, you can live your life however you wish.

And let go of all the bad feelings you may have towards certain people. Take time to go as back as you can remember in your past and forgive anyone who did something hurtful to you.
- Forgive people who bullied you or laughed at you.
- Forgive friends who weren't good friends.
- Forgive your parents if you feel they did something that negatively affected you.

- Forgive people who cheated on you, spoke to you badly, or made you feel bad.
- Forgive anyone who was ever rude to you.

Forgiveness is one of the most liberating feelings, because holding on to negative emotions cripples you.

Someone once said: "feeling resentment towards a person is like drinking poison and expecting that person to die".

Try to imagine these scenarios where negative feelings are poison:

1. One person cuts in front of you at the supermarket. You tell them their gesture was inconsiderate, but they react disrespectfully. You get affected by their attitude, go home, run to the poison cupboard, drink the poison, and wait for the person who upset you at the supermarket to die.
2. Your work colleague took credit for your project, leaving you looking inefficient. So, you run to the poison cupboard, drink the poison, and wait for the selfish colleague to die.
3. You remember a friend who wronged you in high school and to whom you stopped talking ever since. You get angry only thinking of

her. You've drunk so much poison over the years, holding on to the resentment. Today, she came to your mind again, so you ran to the poison cupboard, drank the poison, and waited for her to die.

4. The boyfriend who cheated on you ten years ago deserves some punishment! You haven't forgotten about his betrayal. Again, run to the poison cupboard, drink the poison, and wait for him to die!

Imagine that, whenever someone upsets you, you run to the poison cupboard and drink some poison, waiting for that someone to die.

It's not going to happen! Most people who upset you don't care how they made you feel! So let go of the negative feelings! Stop drinking the poison!

Let go of any resentment and bad feelings you ever felt towards anyone. Not for them, but for yourself! Don't cripple yourself with hostile feelings, thinking you are punishing them!

They live their lives unaffected by the poison YOU choose to drink. And you damage yourself with every sip.

Put the poison down and live a free life!

After forgiving everyone in your life, start being grateful for everything you have:
- your senses
- your body
- the people you love
- the possessions you have
- the experiences you lived
- the lessons you learned
- the ability to open your mind to read this

And now, because your mind is healed and clear, start manifesting! Your aspirations should be colossal! Because there is no one else in your head to dictate how big you should dream. You can visualise the body you want, the job you want, the people you want around you, and the life you want.

AND START TAKING STEPS TOWARDS TURNING YOUR DREAMS INTO REALITY!

TO SUM UP:
- Create good habits to replace the bad ones
- Seek therapy to heal your mind
- Forgive everyone who ever wronged you in any way

- Don't hold grudges or resentments because it's damaging to YOU
- Clear all blockages, so you can progress
- Meditate, listen to mantras, use visualisation technics
- Practice gratitude for everything you have
- Manifest your dreams and start taking action

~ 7 ~

RICH MINDSET

In the book "Rich Dad, Poor Dad," Robert Kiyosaki explains how two fathers' lives were shaped by their respective mindsets regarding money and wealth. And the advice they gave their children was based on how each regarded money and wealth.

Poor Dad believed in studying hard and getting an education to secure a well-paid job.
Rich Dad believed in financial education and learning how to make your money work for you.

Poor Dad would dismiss an opportunity, saying it was too bad he couldn't afford the thing he wanted.
Rich Dad would welcome a challenge and try to find ways to enable him to afford what he wanted.

Poor Dad blamed any financial struggles on the economy and the job market.
Rich Dad believed people's fear and ignorance were the causes of their financial struggles.

Poor Dad saw working for an employer as a safe source of income.
Rich Dad was encouraging financial independence by starting a business.

Two different fathers were teaching their sons lessons, through different mindsets.

A poor mindset is what most people have.
People with a poor mindset are interested in securing a job and having a safe income (maybe getting a few pay raises) until they reach retirement age to enjoy their pension.

An abundant mindset is what wealthy people have.
People with an abundant mindset are interested in making money and putting their money to work, making even more money.

They look for opportunities and take them. They don't fear failure because they understand every failure has lessons to be learned, and they never stop fighting for their goals.
People with a wealthy mindset don't settle. They are visionaries, their dreams are significant, and they want to leave a legacy.

If you hope to become a wealthy person, learn to have a rich person's mindset, even before you start mixing with the rich. But be careful, as building an abundant mindset doesn't mean being irresponsible with your spending habits! Wealthy people buy loads of things because they make back quickly whatever they spend. But they would never spend more than they earn. Rich people don't live beyond their means. So, don't think that a wealthy mindset means reckless spending!

An abundant mindset is about planning, looking for opportunities, taking action, building momentum, and making things happen.

Start building a good relationship with money by planning and understanding your financial situation. Then, using a spreadsheet, keep track of your monthly income and expenses. It's straightforward and will give you an idea about the money going into your bank account and the money leaving it. You will find plenty of tutorials online to help create a personal budget spreadsheet.

Plan for essentials first and non-essentials afterwards.

Your essentials are food, accommodation, bills, and travel. Non-essentials are all the other things and services you buy (but which you can easily adjust if your financial situation changes).

These are a few examples of how to make adjustments to your non-essential spending:
- if you go shopping every time there is a sale, stop buying unnecessary items and look only for things you need
- if you order a lot of takeaways, start cooking at home
- if you blow-dry your hair at the salon too often, invest in a good blow-drier and learn how to do it yourself at home
- if you spend too much on going out, start having drinks at home with friends instead

If you can't reduce the spending on your essentials, you can find ways to reduce the cost of your non-essentials.

START SAVING - YOU WILL SURVIVE!

Top up your savings account regularly. At least 10% of your monthly earnings should go into your savings account, regardless of your income. That percentage should increase once you start earning more, but, for now, learn to put aside at least 10%.

You may think your current situation only allows you to live paycheck to paycheck, and it may seem impossible to survive without the 10%. But if you try for six months to take a chunk of your income and put it away, you will see that, somehow, you will manage to adjust.

EARN MORE

Don't roll your eyes at the idea, as if it is impossible to earn more. It may seem impossible because you've probably never tried to do something to increase your income.

So, if you are happy to moan about all the misfortunes stopping you from changing your circumstances, carry on doing just that: roll your eyes and moan.

But if you are serious about earning more, find a part-time activity to supplement your income.

I must emphasise the importance of keeping all your ventures decent and moral. Never do anything in life that makes you feel ashamed or undignified.

If you feel you don't earn enough and you want to earn extra income, you can:
- take on extra shifts at your work
- join a multi-level marketing business
- provide driving, babysitting or dog-walking services
- organise parties and events
- babysit
- pet sit
- house sit
- bake and sell
- be a part-time PA for a local person
- become a virtual PA
- provide typing services
- sell photos, footage clips and illustrations on Shutterstock or other similar providers
- sell on Amazon, eBay or any other platforms
- do social media and advertising for various organisations
- create and sell merchandise
- etc

Naysayers are mediocre and unsuccessful, so don't disregard the above jobs if you want to earn more. And don't think negatively about money!

If you believe money is the root of all your problems, you will make it the root of your problems.
If you focus on the lack of money, you will attract lack of money.

So instead, focus on attracting more money.
Imagine money coming to you from various sources.
Visualise how you feel when money comes to you.
See yourself with the people with whom you will share your good fortune.
Visualise what you'll buy, where you'll travel etc.

Try! There is nothing complicated about closing your eyes and imagining living the life of your dreams.

I am sure you have already spent much time imagining the worst scenarios. So, for a change, try imagining the best scenario!

And as you visualise an abundant life, **START ACTING TOWARDS MAKING THAT GOAL POSSIBLE!** With your dream continuously in your mind, take the first step! Do something you haven't done before!

Put in the work; otherwise, things will not fall on your lap!

You will not see wealthy people complaining about a lack of money. It's not because they have it, and they have nothing about which to complain.

It's because they have a different mindset.

While a poor mindset focuses on lack, a rich mindset focuses on money-making opportunities.

Instead of focusing on things you don't have, concentrate on everything you have and be grateful for how they've enriched your life. Gratitude is the best way of feeling good and letting go of negative emotions.

Do you know why every self-help book discusses gratitude before manifesting your dreams?
Because when you are grateful, you are in the most blissful state.

You can only bring yourself to that state when you start feeling grateful for the essential things:

- for seeing
- for tasting
- for smelling
- for hearing
- for talking
- for walking
- for the people you love
- for your pets
- for having enough food
- for having clean water
- for living in a free world

Imagine one of those things taken away from you, and your world would shatter.

Do this exercise: stay silent and be grateful for the abovementioned things. Take time to understand the importance of each of them and thank whomever you wish: a higher entity, the Universe, the destiny. It doesn't matter what you believe in. It doesn't even matter if you are a non-believer. You can thank yourself. But allow the feeling the gratitude to spread in every fibre of your being and identify all the sensations. You will see that your senses are much sharper. You will FEEL differently.

If you do this gratitude exercise mindfully and correctly, you should be inundated with warmth and bliss. It will be impossible to experience negative feelings while you are in a state of gratitude. This blissful inner warmth is what you should feel when you manifest your dreams.

Manifesting when your mind is not in a blissful state is not effective. You will only attract what you feel.

All self-help books mention gratitude because only gratitude can bring your mind and body to the most favourable environment.

When your mind is in its optimal state, it signals your body to feel bliss, your vibrations rise, and your mind becomes fertile soil where you can plant your seeds. Your seeds are your dreams.

If you want to grow a bountiful garden, you don't plant on infertile soil, do you? Instead, you first nourish the soil, bring it to its best state, and then, you plant the seeds.

Start respecting and admiring rich people instead of expressing negative feelings towards them. You attract not only what you say but also what you feel and think.

When you free your mind of blockages, including blockages you may have about money, a shift will happen inside you. When that happens, you will recognise it, because it will feel like a weight has lifted from your shoulders. So, seek to reach that state of mind.

***

If you are not a fan of spiritually-based practices, my advice is to do whatever feels right for you. If you think you are happy with everything in your life and stumbled across this book by mistake or started reading it as a laugh, then have your laugh and continue to live your life in bliss.

But if you want to make changes, and one of the changes is exploring the spiritual side, start doing it, because it may be an enlightening experience.

***

Research and study as many sources as possible to learn how to clear any obstructions of energy, including blockages that may prevent money flow.

Our life experiences affect us positively or negatively. And sometimes, you may not be aware of something that your subconscious mind may have picked up in childhood, youth, or even adulthood.

- You may have seen your parents struggle when you were little or heard them talking badly about money and rich people.
- Perhaps you are surrounded by friends who are always complaining about money.
- Maybe you read with regularity news about calamities and watch TV shows about poverty and scarcity.

STOP!

- Stop watching tragic news every day or long-running soaps and TV shows set in disadvantaged areas where everyone struggles. Your mind doesn't know the difference between reality and fiction. Therefore, exposing it to insufficiency and misfortune, your brain picks up on your feelings and forms your reality.

- Spend less time with people who complain about money problems and spend more time in the company of people excited about creating opportunities!

- Watching years of TV shows in deprived areas affects your mindset, so switch to watching success stories instead!

- Keeping up to date with the current news is smart. But reading every tragic story, catastrophic event, and crisis from ten different sources is unnecessary.

- Avoid saying things like "Money doesn't buy happiness" and "I don't care about money." If you say it all the time, your subconscious mind will start associating money with something outside your sphere of interest, and it will keep money far from your reality.

- Build awareness to notice your actions that may block the money flow. When you become more aware of your words and habits, you will understand what is affecting you negatively and begin to change those things and practices. And as discussed in the MIND chapter, you should be aware of your thoughts regarding money, health, relationships, and career.

A healthy mindset should become part of your new lifestyle. Because having a healthy mindset **only occasionally** (but the rest of the time, you still say and do things that harm your relationship with money) is not beneficial in the long term. **You must always be mindful and have the right mindset about everything in your life!**

And you know what other things happen when your mindset changes?

- You will no longer want to be around someone who moans and complains about money.

- You will not seek to watch news about the economic crisis, depression, and market collapse.

- Instead, you will want to read about industries that flourished during the crisis and start-ups that created plenty of jobs and were incredibly lucrative.

- You will seek positive news, and you will feel admiration for people who have ideas and the courage to pursue their dreams.

- Your mind will be drawn only towards success and abundance.

"As humans, we have the amazing ability to change past conditioning. We can achieve this by releasing negativity, interacting with like-minded, conscious people, enjoying inspirational sights and sounds, and engaging in uplifting activities." ~ Deepak Chopra

To help change your mindset, you must not allow external factors to harm your subconscious mind.

- Listen to audiobooks on finance and on how to succeed in business.
- Read success stories.
- Seek abundance in your surroundings: in nature, in the places you go, in the people you meet, and in all the things you watch and hear.

It takes work to shift the paradigm of your mind. Changing bad habits and toxic thoughts, which you've probably had for years, is difficult. Therefore, you must pour abundance into your subconscious mind through all your senses: sight, hearing, smell, taste, and touch.

- Go to the park and watch the abundance of colours, hear the sounds, and smell the aromas around you.
- Watch and be amazed by the glorious sky and majestic architecture.
- Have a coffee in the most expensive hotel. Enjoy the atmosphere, watch the people around and be grateful for having coffee in such luxurious surroundings.
- Find YouTube videos with compilations of images of beautiful holiday destinations, on a background of uplifting music and positive affirmations flashing on the screen. Having these videos running on a TV or laptop screen (in a small window) while doing other things is an excellent way to boost your mood.
- Remember that you should only have the videos running in the background if you are doing things that don't require much concentration. Don't create a distraction for yourself if you need to study or are at work.

- Write down your goals and record yourself while reading them on repeat for 10 – 20 minutes and listen to the recording daily. Ideally, when you wake up and when you go to sleep.
- Live your life in awe of your surroundings.

Pay attention to the above points and put them into practice regularly. It trains your mind to see beauty and plentifulness.

A paradigm is a thought system that drives our habits. If your mind was exposed to bad news, lack and scarcity for many years, you formed your reality based on those.

Now, it's time to shift your paradigm so you can change your mindset and, ultimately, your reality. Autosuggestion, positive affirmations and visualisation are the first steps. And then, be proactive and start working towards your goal!

CREATE VISION BOARDS

Write down your goals, collect pictures from magazines and the Internet, print them out, and place them on a vision board.

Thoughts do become things. But if your thoughts and dreams are not clear and well defined, if you don't "see" them, "smell" them, and "taste" them, if you don't "hear" your dreams "talking" to you daily, they will get lost in your mind's depth!

Do you know how many people will tell you that this is nonsense?
Probably most of them!

Do you know how many of those people feel fully accomplished and happy?
Probably none of them!

Don't let **their** beliefs affect **your** decisions!

Many successful people have vision boards: **Simon Cowell, Oprah Winfrey, Steve Harvey, Ellen DeGeneres, Beyonce, Katy Perry, Jim Carrey**, etc. Are these people successful enough for you to be convinced? Or you're going to ignore the concept because someone (who is not particularly successful) thinks it's "silly"?

To achieve a rich person's mindset, you must flood your mind with so much positive information that your old ideas will become obsolete.

So, don't listen to anyone telling you that making plans, writing down your dreams and creating vision boards is nonsense. Instead, you must do everything you can to help shift your paradigm.

But remember: just a vision board, without putting in the work, is not enough to fulfil your dreams! You must follow the whole plan and complete all the steps.

~ 9 ~

YOUR CIRCLE

You may have to give up two-thirds of the people in your life. They say you must stick with family, no matter what, but at least eliminate toxic friends and friends who drag you down; because people who do not help you grow should not take up too much of your time.

If you have friends who don't progress, see them only occasionally. Be selective with those you give much time and attention to, as they can influence your development and, ultimately, your future.

You need to make space for new people and events, so clear your schedule and limit the time spent with people who cannot add value to your life. They don't need to know about your plan. You can tell them that you are working on an important project, so you won't be able to see anyone at short notice or unplanned.

If people get upset, it's not a problem. Really! You don't need to please everyone. So, at times, it is OK to say No.

You must set boundaries because, although very underrated, time is unbelievably valuable.

As we've learned in a previous chapter, you can lose things and get them back. With time, however, it's different. You don't get it back. So, start giving your time the value that it's worth.

Rich people know how valuable their time is and don't waste it. That's why, whenever someone asks for an appointment, the rich person will ask: "How long will this take?" Because they need to know how much time they will lose if the meeting doesn't benefit them.

Start thinking like a rich person and start valuing your time!

They say you become the average of the five people you spend the most time with.

Look at the five people with whom you spend most of your time. Are they helping your development? Do they inspire you with their success, healthy lifestyle, and inner peace? Are they happy? Do they focus on their growth? Are they charitable?

If the answers are mostly negative, you need to start spending less time with these people and people of this kind.

When telling them you will see them less, you should expect that some may get upset. But you will find that you can live without seeing those friends frequently. And they can live without seeing you so often, as well.

If you have dinner once a month and give them your undivided attention for a couple of hours, you will enjoy each other's company much more. Perhaps the friend who constantly moans about her lazy partner will want to discuss something more interesting if she sees you less.

And it makes financial sense, as you will save money by having drinks at home occasionally, instead of going out all the time.

It is more important to start going where wealthy people go rather than wasting your time and money in places where you will never meet high-calibre people. So, start saving time and money and go where the wealthy frequent!

Take advantage of all opportunities! It's essential to be in the right place at the right time.

And the right place will NOT be a little Chinese restaurant under a bridge in the suburbs...

The right place will be the lounge of a 5-star hotel. Have a coffee there!
The right place will be at an annual art fair. Purchase a ticket!

The right place will be in a designer store at the launch of a new collection. Get yourself invited!

When old friends want to see you, plan a date, and have them around for dinner; give them an evening of your undivided attention and then, carry on with your transformation.

To elevate your life, you must change many things in your routine, which will upset some people. But if you don't deliberately hurt someone, you shouldn't stop yourself from working towards your dreams.

A natural selection will occur within the people of your circle; you should just let it happen. Don't try to hang on to people when you are growing. We all have our paths to follow.

This book is a journey of educating yourself, so have an honest introspective and try to identify if you picked up any bad habits from your old friends. If you did, eliminate such habits and continue your journey with a positive mind, respect for your time and high standards regarding who will become part of your new circle.

MOVE WHERE THE AFFLUENT PEOPLE LIVE

If not immediately, then later in the future, when it's possible, you must move to an affluent area.

Living in a disadvantaged area makes the chances of meeting wealthy people exceedingly small. But living in an affluent neighbourhood can make it possible to bump into rich people everywhere: on the street, in the local park, at the supermarket, in a coffee shop, at the gym, at a local event etc. So you need to be where they are to increase your chances of making acquaintances among the rich.

You may befriend your neighbour, and they may introduce you to a relative who is a great guy but works too much and doesn't have time to go out and meet women.

You may discover that the guy who walks his dog in the park every Saturday is single and noticed you.

You will begin to recognise the locals' faces on the street and then start chatting, and you may eventually have a coffee together and form friendships. They will then introduce you to their friends, and their friends will introduce you to their friends, which will expand your networking web.

You will attend local events, which are great for networking and being introduced to the neighbourhood.

Living where rich people live will give you access to them, so use some of your spare time to visit new places and meet new people.

Even if you don't necessarily want to meet someone with whom to be in a romantic relationship, you will meet new people with different perspectives on life. They may be very well-read or well-travelled and inspire you with their knowledge.

One thing guaranteed when living in a wealthy neighbourhood is that you can learn from successful people how to become calmer, more generous, polite and diplomatic.

If you stroll in an affluent area, you will be aware of a certain vibe which makes you feel good. The surroundings are grander. People are more relaxed and kinder.

Strangers smile, nod and compliment you, and the energy exuded from them and all the beautiful things you see around fill you with an exhilarating joy.

After experiencing and getting used to this vibe, you will want more. That is when you know you will do everything you can to live in a place that makes you feel so good.

Start cutting some people from your life, and don't worry about how you will be perceived! It's time to think about your future. Of course, you will try and make that change gently because your intention is not to hurt your friends. But if someone gets upset, it's their choice to do so. Be polite, but don't bring your plan to a halt just because someone in your life may not like that you will allocate less time for them in future. Let them deal with their issues; you cannot be everyone's saviour.

NOTES:
• Cut as many people as necessary out of your life
• Keep only 1/3 of the people who are most important to you
• Revaluate friendships and relationships
• Study the five people with whom you spend the most time and make notes of their behaviour

• Make sure you get rid of any bad habits that you may have picked up from others
• Don't waste too much time doing mediocre things
• Use your time wisely
• Schedule meetings with your friends and allocate them a limited time
• Tell family and friends that you will be busy with a new project
• Free time for upcoming events and the new people in your life

~ 11 ~

YOUR INCOME

To do this project correctly, you will need a decent income. Therefore, it is essential not only to have a good mindset about money and abundance but also to be wise with your spending and the money you make.

You don't necessarily need a very highly-paid job.
But you do need to:
- **make a decent living**
- **save up**
- **invest in yourself**

You may have to take up a second job temporarily, so your income allows you to be in places where you can mix with the rich. You can learn hacks to do this project on a budget, but you must master applying those hacks so that you do not display any traces of desperation; otherwise, you will not succeed. Desperation is not attractive!

Wealthy people will NOT be put off by someone who has a simple but decent job or works two jobs to earn extra money. If anything, they will be impressed with you. So don't be ashamed to work! Most men see independence as sexy. And exuding sexiness through confidence is infinitely better than trying to be sexy by displaying an inappropriate amount of flesh in public.

If you do need to get a temporary second job, this could be:
- babysitting
- housesitting
- pet sitting
- pet grooming
- dog walking
- delivery
- taxi driving
- shopping
- doing odd jobs
- joining a multi-level marketing company

- selling things on eBay
- making cakes or art and crafts and selling them to your local market
- catering
- personal assistant
- virtual assistant
- managing social media for businesses
- tutoring
- personal training
- translating
- running errands for people
- home organising
- freelance bookkeeping
- party organising
- party entertaining
- photography selling
- becoming a mystery shopper
- taking online surveys
- copywriting
- copy-editing
- researching
- recruiting
- etc

Don't turn your nose up at these jobs. Instead, consider them as a temporary solution to increase your income. You need to be able to afford to be in places where the wealthy go. In later chapters, you will see that it will not cost you a fortune, but you can't expect to do it without any money.

Find social platforms, websites, apps and groups where to place ads offering your services for part-time jobs you think you can do in your spare time.

I must emphasise that this book teaches you how to meet and date a wealthy man, but this doesn't necessarily mean that the first wealthy man you'll meet will be the one taking you down the aisle.

It is possible to meet your dream man very quickly and for both of you to fall in love. But you may meet a few men before finding the one destined to be with you. Just be patient!

In the meantime, you must strive to raise your standards. And while going through your transformation, you will notice that you will learn to enjoy an elevated lifestyle. After you experience that lifestyle, you will not want to go back to dating men with modest incomes. And not because you expect the men you date to give you an expensive lifestyle, but because you will discover that, with effort and ambition, you can achieve that lifestyle on your own.

And because you CAN achieve it alone, you will be much more selective about the kind of men you will be interested in romantically.

Taking on a project like this does not mean you should do it without love. So go ahead, fall in love and experience romance, because many wealthy men are romantics who appreciate and love women. But take your time and find a good man! Don't settle for less!

Don't be afraid to aspire to meet someone of a high calibre just because you have a low-paid job. A classy, generous rich man will not make you feel inadequate if you don't earn as much as him.

And if you have dreams, share them with him, and you will find that the right kind of man will gladly help you in your journey to achieve your goals.

This book doesn't teach you to be a kept woman or a sugar babe. On the contrary, it teaches you to become independent, while acknowledging that being with a man who can help you achieve your dreams is OK.

Therefore, it is essential to start planning your future and act towards your goals, so you can learn to become a wealthy woman in your own right.

Being among wealthy people will convince you that if you like their kind of life and aspire to an elevated lifestyle, you must start working towards becoming someone who can afford that lifestyle, with or without a man.

Therefore, after the transformation, some women may soon meet someone they like. While for others, it may be a shift in their mindset where WEALTH and SUCCESS will be up there alongside LOVE on their list of priorities. So, when they ponder their next relationship, they will immediately know they want the type of man who achieved material success. And it's nothing wrong with wanting a high-standard man!

This book doesn't teach you to be a kept woman! Instead, it teaches you to value yourself and want more from life, romance, and the man with whom you share the romance.

So, if you are already in a good relationship with an ambitious man starting to build wealth, do not leave that man for someone you may think is better! Instead, support each other and reach a fulfilling life together!

But if you are a single woman wanting to find romance, level up and raise your standards. Just keep in mind that the type of man you want to meet is in a smaller pool of people, and the competition is fierce, so be smart and don't rush the process!

Read, RE-READ, learn and apply the rules from every chapter to elevate yourself and your standards.

In your journey to meet high-calibre people, you must not compromise your reputation by doing something out of desperation and regretting it afterwards. So don't get yourself involved in anything disgraceful.

You must remain classy throughout!

NOTES:
- Make a decent living
- If needs be, take up a second job, even if it's a part-time activity
- Learn to like high standards and work to afford the high standards
- If you are single, choose a high-value man
- If you are in a relationship with an ambitious man, support each other and build a good life together
- Read, RE-READ and follow the plan, step by step

- Be a decent, clean-living individual!

~ 12 ~

WHAT AGE AND SIZE DO YOU NEED TO BE TO BAG A MILLIONAIRE?

This chapter (and others which will follow) will upset some people, so if you are uninterested in the transformation, you can stop reading now.

The good news is that there is no age limit, provided you are over 18! So, whether you are 20, 30, 40, 50, 60 or older, the age doesn't matter. There are millionaire men out there for women of all ages.

However, if you are 40, you must be a young 40.
If you are 50, you must be a young 50.
If you are 60, you must be a young 60.

What does that mean?

It means that you must be someone who ages gracefully and has a healthy glow at any age.

I am sure you know women who do not show their age because they look after their skin, hair, weight, and general appearance. Aspire to become like those women!

It's wrong to think that ALL millionaires prefer young women because it's not always true!

If a young guy dates a young woman, it is appropriate. But if a man in his 50s or 60s is only interested in 20-year-old women, I can assure you that you don't need to waste your time with this man!

Fortunately, there are many gentlemen out there. Many mature men like mature women. And there are rich men for women of all ages.

Be charming and classy!
People will be drawn to you if they feel good around you, not if you are a 50-year-old woman who dresses like a teenager. That kind of behaviour may bring people to you for the wrong reasons. You certainly don't want that! You want to become the woman who exudes charm and class through every pore, whether you are 20 or 60. And you want to make people feel at ease in your presence. Become the woman men want to be with and women want to be like!

Aspire to inspire!
Look after yourself so that you can age gracefully and you will be attractive at any age.
Learn to be elegant and feminine, and you will be attractive at any age.
Learn good manners, and you will be attractive at any age.
Love life and live your life gently and appropriately, and you will be attractive at any age.

***

The bad news is that this project is NOT for women with weight problems: very large women or very thin women.

Why?
Because in both cases, being very underweight or very overweight is an evident health issue. And if a rich man is not intrigued by you when he first sees you, it rarely happens later.

What is a healthy-looking figure?
* A healthy-looking figure is anything from a UK size 8 to a UK size 12.
(Of course, size 6 can be an exception, if the woman is petite. In which case, a UK size 6 can also be healthy, but the body frame

matters significantly. She must be petite. If she is tall and size 6, she may look too thin.)

Maintaining an elegant appearance can be challenging for women above UK size 12. A larger woman (UK size 14 or over) CAN look elegant **sometimes**, but she CAN NOT always look elegant. And possessing constant elegance is what you want to achieve from the beginning of your transformation. So, you must look graceful in your clothes, no matter what you wear.

You want your clothes to fit you well.
You want to walk and move gracefully.
You want to look stylish and refined.
And you cannot do all these if you are overweight or underweight.

Why?
Because when you are heavier, your poise is compromised.
Because if you are too skinny or too heavy, you will not wear your clothes with the same elegance. You may dress for your size, but you will not necessarily be able to hide the weight.

Have you ever wondered why most spouses of rich men and most women in the public eye are between sizes UK 8 and UK 12?

It's because sizes 8 to 12 are generally considered healthy-looking and attractive. And if these women (of a certain status) lose or gain too much weight, they seek help.

Most wealthy women don't let themselves jump from a size 8 to a size 16 without doing anything about it. If size 16 would feel and look so wonderful, they would happily remain larger. But they KNOW that the clothes don't look as good on them, the walking and the moving are not as graceful, and their general health and appearance are compromised.

So, make sure that, before you apply the next steps of your transformation, you deal with the size issue first. A healthy-looking size is between UK size 8 and UK size 12. (A UK size 6 can also be healthy IF you are petite and have a small frame. However, a UK size 6 can be too skinny if you are of average height or tall.)

And yes, some men prefer large women or very skinny women, but these are rare, so I am eliminating the extremes. The book covers the most met wealthy individuals, so I keep the desired weight brackets between 8 and 12 (UK sizes). If you are skinnier than UK size 8 or larger than UK size 12, speak to a nutritionist to start a diet which will make you look healthy.

I am sure this will not go down well with many people because we live in a society obsessed with promoting women of all sizes, and it's OK to do so, but the book is about how to elevate yourself and date a high-calibre man. So, to complete this project successfully, you must start getting into shape. Finding a wealthy man who wants to be with you would be much more challenging if you don't have a healthy weight.

What is a healthy weight?
Calculate your Body Mass Index (BMI). According to the World Health Organization (WHO):

- A BMI of less than 18.5 means a person is underweight.
- A BMI of between 18.5 and 24.9 is the ideal weight.
- A BMI of between 25 and 29.9 means a person is overweight.
- A BMI over 30 indicates obesity.

You can find BMI calculators online, in pharmacies, at your doctor's practice, and in health clubs or gyms. There are no excuses for you not to know your BMI!

The ideal weight is the weight suggested by all the health organisations in the world. So, if the BMI reading indicates you are underweight or overweight, it's true!

You may believe society body-shames you, but your BMI is not body-shaming you! Trust the readings and, if necessary, do something about it. Your ideal BMI is what helps you obtain optimal health.

A weight issue is not primarily about physical attractiveness.
It's about health!
And you should care about your health even if you don't care about being with a wealthy man. **You should care about your health if you want to live a happy life!**

And yes, wealthy men prefer women who look healthy and elegant.

I know some plus-size models and celebrities look fabulous in their outfits. But these women have their clothes made for them, and when something is bespoke, it fits and looks great. But, unfortunately, it's also a costly affair. So, your size must be one that allows you to find ready-to-wear clothes to make you look presentable.

If you are within the sizes mentioned above, then great! Keep a healthy diet and maintain that size. Maintaining the same size over the years will make wearing elegant clothes effortless. And if you need clarification on what constitutes a nutritious diet, research or speak to a nutritionist.

Generally, a healthy diet is based mainly on vegetables, fruits, nuts, seeds, whole grains, fish and very little meat and dairy. If you follow a colourful diet and exercise regularly, you can maintain a healthy and attractive figure.

You don't need to be a gym enthusiast and have six-pack abs to be attractive. However, a gentleman appreciates a lady who looks after her figure because he also looks after his.

A gentleman would not necessarily find a gym freak very stimulating, especially if the only topics of every discussion are fitness, diet and nutrition. It's nothing wrong with being a gym enthusiast, but don't turn into a freak! Otherwise, you can only attract another gym freak. And not all gym freaks are wealthy.

Rich men have access to exquisite beauty in various forms: from material things to destinations, food, and people. Therefore, if you want to have a chance to be of interest to wealthy gentlemen, you must learn to look and behave the part, because the majority will go for someone who is healthy-looking and exquisite in every way.

And while most rich men prefer healthy-looking women, not all rich men are interested in 20-year-old women. So don't eliminate yourself from the process because you are 40, 50 or 60 or over! **Many men indeed like youth, but even more men love sophistication.**

A wealthy mature gentleman will look for a sophisticated mature woman. Older men who want to date very young women are sleazy, and you don't want to find that type of rich man anyway!

There are young wealthy men for young women and mature ones for mature women. Choose for your age and remain dignified.

In conclusion, in this journey to find a wealthy man, AGE DOES NOT MATTER (if you are over 18). But SIZE DOES MATTER, so keep it between UK size 8 and UK size 12 (unless you are petite - in which case you can look healthy as a UK size 6, too).

NOTES:
• You can be any age over 18 (as long as you age gracefully)
• You can only be between UK size 8 to UK size 12 (check the size chart of your country, as the measures may be different)
• UK size 6 may be an exception only if you are petite, but not if you are of average height or tall (otherwise, you would be too skinny)
• Exercise, but don't turn into a gym freak
• Keep a healthy diet so that you can maintain a healthy and attractive figure
• Dress and behave for your age
• "Fish" from the appropriate age pond

~ 13 ~

HAIR

The hair must be clean, glossy, bouncy, and preferably long. But be careful with the length of your hair! Your hair can not go below your elbows; otherwise, you'll fall into the opposite category: looking unkempt. **Long hair is beautiful, but hair too long is not attractive!**

Start an intensive hair treatment through a healthy diet if your hair is not thriving. Eat more avocado, eggs, nuts, seeds, oily fish, shellfish, whole grains, and green vegetables, which are great for hair. Have regular health check-ups to ensure you take the necessary supplements if you have any vitamin deficiencies. Be aware of any allergies and intolerances.

Your hair must smell divine, ALWAYS! And you can only have divine-smelling hair by washing it daily. Sometimes, even if the tips of your hair smell nice, your scalp may be foul-smelling because we all sweat when we sleep. And although you may not be aware of any unpleasant odour coming from your scalp, someone with a keen sense of smell will know if your hair hasn't been washed for a few days.

It doesn't matter what anyone tells you: rarely can you go one day without washing your hair, if you want it to smell and look at its best.

To test if your scalp smells clean, rub the tips of your fingers vigorously on your scalp for 30 seconds and smell your fingers. You may be surprised at what you find. Imagine a man wanting to bury his nose in your hair and inhale that scent!

You may ask why it is essential for the scalp to smell nice because it is not like the first millionaire you will meet will sniff your scalp. That is indeed very unlikely. However, for someone with a sharp sense of smell, in your vicinity, a gust of wind through your hair will be enough to make or break that first impression. Trust me - I have been near people with smelly scalps. It was unpleasant!

Whenever I could smell the sweat coming from someone's scalp, I was left disappointed no matter how good-looking the person was. And I didn't need to be too close to them either; smell travels.

Yes, daily washing your hair may not be advisable, but if you want to give your hair a break occasionally, do it when you stay home. Don't go out to meet people with unwashed hair!

Your hairdresser will most likely advise you not to wash your hair daily, and you should listen to their advice! But when you meet people, your hair must be impeccable, if you want to look and feel confident.

Your hair should look perfect every time you go out to make connections, even if the intention is not necessarily to meet a man.

Everyone you meet can play an essential part in your future, so make sure you look presentable when you meet high-calibre people.

Have your days off when you give your hair a break and an intense treatment. But don't go out looking unkempt and ruin your chances when meeting high-quality people. Only if you look flawless and behave exquisitely will you become memorable.

The tips of your hair must be trimmed regularly, and never allow them to become split or dry. Learn to look after your hair as thoroughly as you do with your general health, because untidy-looking hair ruins your overall image.

If you dye your hair, your roots can never show, so do not overlook that aspect! Especially if the contrast between your hair's natural colour and the colour of your hair dye is evident.

Roots of a different colour are not trendy! On the contrary, they are unsightly and unclassy.

You can find natural hair dyes on the market that are safe to use every few weeks to maintain even colour coverage.

Also, keep the colour as natural as possible. Whether you are a blonde, a brunette or a redhead, your chosen colour must have a natural shade.

The **blonde** should not be yellow! Lovely shades of blonde are champagne blonde, creamy blonde, summer blonde, buttermilk blonde, light golden, sandy blonde, honey blonde, chestnut blonde, and caramel blonde.

Platinum, silver, pearl or white are not colours you can wear daily! Those colours may look good in adverts but not on young women.

If you are an older woman with naturally grey hair and don't want to dye it, it's OK to keep that natural shade of grey but maintain your hair nicely styled, well-conditioned and glossy. In this case, grey hair can look nice, but it needs to be very well looked after.

However, silver hair doesn't look right if you are in your 20s.

Most shades of **brown** look natural, but ensure your brown hair is not dull. Get advice from a few hairstylists on what shade of brown to choose, what highlights (if necessary) and how to keep your hair glossy.

If you want to be a **redhead**, go for shades closer to ginger, copper and auburn and avoid bright colours, such as scarlet red, raspberry red, mahogany, or cherry red. These are not natural hair colours and may look good on the box but not on you.

Any unusual hair colour may look beautiful when you leave the hairdresser, but it's unlikely that your hair will look good when you style it yourself.

Black hair can look dull if it doesn't reflect light to make it look shiny. So make sure it's well-conditioned and doesn't lose its lustre. If you can't get it to shine, have some highlights illuminating your face.

Finding a colour and a hairstyle that suits you is significant! Also, the hair must be immaculate and healthy-looking when meeting people.

To recap, for your hair to look its best, you must wash it. If you want days off when you give your hair a break from washing, do it on the days you stay home. Then, when you go out, wash and style your hair.

Looking after your hair can be expensive, so you should learn to style it at home. That way, you will always have beautiful hair, not only when you go to the hair salon.

Your hair must look like you came out of the hairdresser every time you are in public. Invest in a good electric hairbrush and use cold air to reduce damage.

If you can, keep your hair long, because most men prefer long hair. Well-groomed long or mid-length hair will get you noticed.

However, a bob may look better for hair that is too fine or frizzy. If your hair is too fine and lacks volume, a longer length will make it look shapeless and boring. On the other hand, if your hair is too frizzy and long, it may look too voluminous and hard to tame. Discuss with the hairstylist, and they'll advise you.

Do not get hair extensions!
Most hair extensions look cheap, and you do not want to suffer a mishap and have any of your extensions break at a very inopportune moment, as it would put off people, especially men.

Hair extensions freak men out. They love the idea of running their fingers through a woman's hair, and if they know that yours may come off is not something they would want to see.

So, if hair extensions freak out most men, what makes you think that a rich man will be attracted to your hair extensions, when there are so many women with beautiful natural hair?

I know that some women have such fine hair that it looks unhealthy. But rather than going for the extensions to add volume, I recommend seeing a hair loss specialist who can advise how to grow healthy hair. You may have to take a treatment, and you may have to change your diet and get rid of your bad habits, but I encourage you to do anything you can to keep your hair natural. **Do not put unnecessary extensions in your hair!**

NOTES:

- Wash and style your hair whenever you go out to meet people
- Keep your hair medium or long, but not below your elbows
- Or have a shorter cut if the hair is too fine or too frizzy

- If you dye your hair, choose a natural-looking colour
- Eat more avocado, eggs, nuts, seeds, oily fish, shellfish, whole grains and green vegetables
- Condition your hair and keep it healthy
- Do not get extensions!

~ 14 ~

EYEBROWS

Never tattoo your eyebrows!

Please note that I am excluding the cases of aesthetic reconstruction following an accident or illness!

If you are from the generation who overplucked and now the eyebrows stopped growing, look for alternatives to regenerate them so they can start growing again. Do not touch them for one, two, or three years if necessary! Do everything you can to recover your eyebrows, but do not run to the tattoo or microblading parlour because classy people find tattooed eyebrows horrifying. You can miss out on great opportunities if you tattoo your face.

The "microblading experts" will tell you that microblading differs from a tattoo. They will try to convince you that, while the tattoo ink develops into blue or green, the pigment they use in microblading fades into a lighter version of the colour they used. That is not true! **The inks used in microblading are similar to the ones used in tattoos**, penetrating the skin deep enough to remain there.

The Internet is full of stories from people sharing their experiences.

The pigment has often changed to orange, green or blue. Some people are happy to tell their stories, so others don't make the same mistake. And you can ask to meet them to see them face to face if you need more convincing.

Don't read only the positive reviews without hearing experiences from people for whom microblading went wrong, because those with positive reviews don't know how their procedure will turn out in a few years. Microblading is still relatively new, but you will hear more and more stories about dissatisfied customers in the years to come.

Also, it doesn't matter if, at the microblading parlour, there are pictures of procedures that look "natural". DO NOT DO IT! They may "look" natural in photos, but it's different when you meet face-to-face with someone who's had the procedure.

And if nothing can convince you not to go ahead with microblading/tattooing your eyebrows, remember that visible tattoos could be obstacles in your elevating process.

It's OK to do as you wish with your body, and you can have as many tattoos as you want. But if you want to be in a relationship with a classy wealthy man, remember that rich men dislike eyebrows drawn with pencil, microbladed or tattooed. So, do not microblade or tattoo your eyebrows if you plan to meet and be with a wealthy man!

It's not to say that you will not get any man if you tattoo your eyebrows. You will get A MAN, but it is doubtful that he will be a high-value man.

Rich men hate tattooed and microbladed eyebrows! Trust me; I asked many!

I've seen women who missed out on opportunities to date wealthy individuals because they had tattooed eyebrows, and that was enough to put men off.

Most wealthy men admit that they dislike hair extensions and tattooed eyebrows.

Just think about it:
Why would a wealthy man be attracted to someone with extensions or tattooed eyebrows when so many women still have natural hair and eyebrows?!

For as long as there are women with natural looks in the world, wealthy men will prefer them to those with fake hair, eyebrows, lips etc.

It doesn't matter what anyone will tell you - tattooed and microbladed eyebrows look unnatural!

Standing close enough to someone with microbladed/tattooed eyebrows, one can see that the dark shadow above their eyes doesn't have hair, and men are freaked out by the hairless shadows above the eyes, where eyebrows should be.

Imagine when the tattoo turns green, blue or orange! Can you blame a man for not being attracted to a woman with green, blue or orange eyebrows?

If they don't hurt anyone and if it's not immoral or illegal, men (just like women) should have the right to feel attracted to whomever they like.

And the wealthy meet a lot of women. But they will be romantically interested in those who are as natural as possible. Unfortunately, women with tattoos on their faces don't fall into that category!

Rich men meet many people through work, social events, travelling or just walking in their neck of the woods. Of those people they meet, many are women, and some are stunning women!

Do you think a rich man will overlook your eyebrows at such an early stage when he can meet so many beautiful women who are natural and refined?

Wealthy men will notice your looks first. If you compromise your appearance, you can still impress them with your intelligence, personality, etc., but they will not be interested in you romantically.

You would not get the chance to get to know the rich man who bumped into you at that event if he noticed your tattooed eyebrows.

The first impression decides your chances, which is why the first impression needs to be excellent.

You may consider this discriminatory and unfair, but it is what it is. And frankly, men (just like women) should be allowed to like what they think is beautiful as long as they don't hurt anyone.

If you tattooed your eyebrows before reading this book and the brows cannot be repaired or saved, you would need to be brilliant in every possible way to get a rich man to overcome that fact. But even so, research and see if you can repair the eyebrows through laser or other methods. Then, invest in correcting them!

Don't leave your eyebrows tattooed, because they will change colour in a few years, and you will regret the decision.

Another reason rich men will not accept going out with women with tattooed eyebrows is because it's not only about what they think.

When they attend events accompanied by women, they consider how they will be perceived by friends, family, business associates, and acquaintances. Yes, rich people care significantly about their image. So besides the fact that tattooed eyebrows freak them out, they don't want others to talk negatively about them and their choices.

And don't try to justify tattooing your face with examples of people for whom microblading/tattooing seemed to have worked.
It is true that Helen Mirren, for example, had her eyebrows done too, and she spoke publicly about how pleased she was with the decision. But Helen Mirren had them done in her 70s.

And in her case, it is understandable. The hair becomes thinner and sparser as we age, and the eyebrow loses its fullness.

Also, Helen Mirren doesn't need to work to attract a rich man. She is an accomplished woman who can do almost anything and will still be attractive.

This advice is for younger women who wish to preserve their natural looks for as long as possible; a natural look and an impeccable image are incredibly attractive.

As I'm sure you know, microbladed eyebrows are also present among the wealthy. I have also seen many rich married women who decided to microblade their eyebrows.

Were their husbands happy with their wives' choices?

Probably not.

But it matters less since those women have already "bagged" their millionaires.

And yes, every woman can do as she wishes with her body.

I just state a fact: on a first impression, between two equally beautiful and intelligent women, the rich guy will prefer the one with natural eyebrows.

Also, do not colour your eyebrows with a black or brown pencil. That is another hideous thing to do to your brows. Eyebrows must be in harmony with the rest of your face, and you should avoid making them your main feature. So, eyebrow makeup is generally unnecessary. You can use a little powder to disguise gaps, but don't start drawing on your skin! You may think your coloured eyebrows look OK in your poorly lit bathroom, but I can reassure you that outside, in the daylight, you look like you've just had your face painted.

Go to a stylist to teach you how to correct gaps in your eyebrows with powder and cosmetics, but try not to use a pencil, as the colour may be too harsh and make you look vulgar.

The shape of the eyebrows should be in harmony with the rest of your face; unfortunately, only a few beauticians know how to shape eyebrows properly. Many beauticians practice this job, but only some understand how to harmonise your face. I advise you to research intensively before allowing someone to touch your eyebrows because the shape of your eyebrows can change your entire face.

NOTES:
• Don't overpluck your eyebrows
• Don't tattoo or microblade your eyebrows
• Don't colour them with pencils
• Find an excellent eyebrow stylist to give you the correct shape for your face

Disclaimer:
Please note that I am excluding the cases of aesthetic reconstruction following an accident or illness!

~ 15 ~

EYES and EYELASHES

For everyday makeup, you can use a little eye pencil to define your eyes but opt for something other than very heavy smokey eyes during the day.

The smokey eye makeup is a look that works only for the evening and only if done in good taste. If you go to lunch with a high-calibre man, he will not find you attractive if you wear your whole palette of eyeshadows. In the evening, you can get away with heavier smokey eyes or some tasteful coloured eye shadows; but during the day, classy men will stay away if your face looks like a Christmas tree.

Day makeup should be discreet and make you look youthful. If your makeup ages you, then you are doing it wrong!

Generally, your whole face makeup should hide a few blemishes, give you a healthy glow and bring out your eyes. That's all daytime makeup should do.

If you draw a thick black line on your bottom eyelid, it will age you.

But if you find a soft eye pencil and draw a fine line on the bottom lid, then dab it to create a shadow rather than a line, it will give the impression that the eyelashes on the lower eyelid are thicker than they are, bringing out your eyes beautifully.

However, on the upper eyelid, where the eyelash curve is, you can draw a darker line because the line will be hidden by the top lashes, making them look thicker. Dab it a little to make the colour uniform, clean any smudges, and apply mascara - this is the most simple and youthful eye makeup.

The older a woman gets, the less eye makeup she should wear.

Instead of that black line on the lower lid's waterline (seen often and very unattractive), you should concentrate more on the top eyelid. If your upper eyelashes look darker than your bottom lashes, it will give you a youthful look. So all you need is some eye pencil on both eyelids (a little amount on the lower lid and a more generous amount on the upper lid), dab it gently, remove any smudges, give it a minute to dry, and then apply the mascara.
Your eyes will look amazing!

Keep your eyelashes natural. Like hair extensions, fake eyelashes may come off at a very inopportune moment, which can be embarrassing for you and off-putting for the people present.

Of course, there are accidents and illnesses when people lose their eyelashes, in which case, an alternative is justified.

But generally, you don't have to wear fake eyelashes unless you are in a photo shoot or film studio and take them off as soon as you finish your photographic or filming session.

Do your research and find the top three mascaras; try them all and stick with the one that works best for you. Always use mascara for daytime and evening. It enhances your eyes, and your face lights up even if you decide not to use any other makeup.

NOTES:
• Don't use bold eyeshadows or smokey eyes during the day
• Use a little bit of eye pencil on your bottom lid and dab it to look more like a shadow than a line
• Darken the eyelashes on your top lid to make your eyes pop
• Use a good quality mascara

• Don't use fake eyelashes (if your eyelashes are not damaged)

Disclaimer:
Please note that there are accidents and illnesses when people lose their eyelashes, in which case fake lashes or other alternatives are justified.

~ 16 ~

LIPS

Lip enhancement procedures may be trendy, but injected lips never look natural. There will always be angles from which they look fake.

So, unless it's a case of aesthetic reconstruction following an accident, illness, or significant congenital disability, I advise leaving your lips natural, just like the rest of you.

Use a lip balm with SPF, so the sun will not damage them and keep them plump, healthy, and moisturised. Don't smoke, as smoking tends to create wrinkles around your mouth, and after many years of smoking, a smoker gets a grey and dull look.

Keep your lips smooth, exfoliate them, stay hydrated, don't let them dry, and wear lipstick (if you want). Or even a tinted lip balm. Also, pale shades of pink, nude or clear lipgloss are beautiful.

Don't go for black lipstick or any other unusual colours. If you are very young and want to experience various lipstick colours, wear them with your friends, but not when you are out and trying to network.

Men like red lipstick, but choose one that doesn't transfer from your lips to your teeth.

Rich men DON'T like:
- women with black, purple, green (or any unusual colour) lipstick
- injected lips which are too obvious
- tattooed lips
- dry lips
- lipstick or lip liner going well above your lips
- lipstick stuck to your teeth

When you contour your lips, don't try and make them look bigger than they are, as it makes you look vulgar. Using a lip liner in a very different colour from your lipstick is considered old-fashioned. And if your lips are not big, the lip liner won't enlarge them.

You are the only one who thinks they look good. On the contrary, they make you look tacky. Stop doing that!

The lip liner's primary role is to keep lipstick or lipgloss in place and to prevent smudging, and it should be the same colour as the lipstick or lipgloss used. And yes, if appropriately applied, it can give the appearance of fuller lips, but my opinion is to keep your makeup simple.

Rather than drawing bigger lips on your face or injecting your lips, use ingredients that may give them some volume.

Cinnamon, menthol and cayenne pepper can have a plumping effect on the lips. But don't apply them directly to your lips, as they may irritate you. Instead, search for lip balms, lip glosses and lipsticks which contain these ingredients and may make your lips appear fuller.

All injected lips look the same. So, dear women with acid injected into the lips, know that your lips look fake from almost every angle!

Therefore, if other women (who may be your competition) have natural lips, they have an advantage over you, even with smaller lips, because **rich men prefer natural lips.**

You have to be exceptional in every way to stand out in a crowd full of fake lips, as rich men will always prefer women who look natural.

And again, if you use lipstick, use only red, nude, clear or light shades of pink.

Black, brown lipstick or any unnatural colours are disliked by men, in general.

NOTES:
- Keep your lips healthy and moisturised
- Don't smoke
- Use a lip balm with SPF
- Use red, pastel pink, nude and clear lipsticks and lipglosses
- Don't use black or other strange colour lipsticks
- Don't use a lip liner or lipstick which goes over the natural lines of your lips
- Don't inject acid into your lips

TEETH

Because the smile is one of the most important things that men immediately notice, bright and white teeth are a great asset.

Bright white teeth and fresh breath indicate good health and are more attractive than any make-up. So, if you want to improve your looks, invest in your smile!

There is nothing sexier to a man than a tidy woman smiling and smelling good!

More daily maintenance than brushing your teeth 2-3 times is required. You should also floss to eliminate any food trapped between your teeth.

Why is it important to floss?
Bacteria will remain where the brush doesn't reach, forming dental plaque. If not removed within 48 hours, dental plaque will harden and calcify, turning into calculus (tartar).

Why is it important to see the hygienist?

Tartar is a cement-like substance that a toothbrush can not remove. Several days of tartar buildup will damage the tooth enamel. Damage to the tooth's enamel may cause cavities and gum irritation. And this can result in gum disease (such as gingivitis and periodontitis).

That's why more measures than brushing your teeth are required for good teeth.

Flossing and regular visits to the hygienist are crucial.
Ideally, see your hygienist every three to six months. A thorough cleaning will eliminate any buildup that can compromise your oral health. And keeping good oral hygiene will benefit your overall health.

Also, consider using mouthwash with essential oils.

Use a tongue scraper to remove any remaining particles on the tongue. Cleaning your tongue will remove bacteria that cause bad breath and improve your tongue's appearance and sense of taste.

Brush, floss, clean your tongue and use mouthwash together, as they all have different functionalities for your mouth's health and hygiene.

Straighten your teeth, if necessary. Braces are not only for children; adults have their teeth straightened too. Wearing braces is not the most attractive thing, but it's temporary. Imagine the beautiful smile and the confidence boost when the braces are removed. Also, if your teeth are only slightly crooked, you could use other orthodontic treatments that don't require wearing braces. Speak to your dentist, who will advise you on the best solution.

If your teeth are beyond repair, consider having cosmetic dentistry. And if the cost is too high, enquire about a payment plan and go for it! Investing in a great set of teeth will be worth every penny, and it's one of the very few cosmetic procedures I recommend.

But, as usual, research before deciding to have something so significant done to your face. Choosing a suitable professional is essential, so take your time and do all the research.

In the meantime, whiten your teeth if they are grey or yellow!
Whitening is relatively inexpensive, and you can find discounts if you look for special offers from dentists in your area. Have your

teeth professionally whitened once, and you can keep them bright forever by using the right products, brushing, flossing and regular hygiene appointments.

If your teeth are naturally white, maintain them with whitening strips and gel.

Always carry with you sugar-free mints. Research which mints are the best options (in terms of ingredients and preferred flavour), and always bring them with you. However, avoid chewing gum! If it happens one day, not to have mints, and a piece of gum is the only option, keep it in your mouth (without chewing it!) to release the flavour and refresh your breath. Then dispose of it discreetly when you feel your breath is fresh.

Never chew gum! Classy women don't chew gum!

NOTES:
• Brush your teeth and gums for two minutes, two-three times a day
• Floss daily
• Use mouthwash
• Scrape your tongue
• Don't smoke
• Limit sugary foods and drinks
• Eat a healthy diet

- Drink plenty of water throughout the day
- Straighten your teeth
- Have a professional teeth whitening treatment
- Then maintain them with whitening strips
- If necessary, consider braces or cosmetic dentistry
- Carry mints with you all the time and use them

~ 18 ~

SKIN

Most of the time, wearing makeup foundation is unnecessary.

If you are not on a movie set or a photo shoot, and if you don't have any blemishes on your skin, the skin foundation is not necessary.

If only minor things need disguising, you can do so by using a little concealer or very lightweight foundation.

If there are significant things that need disguising, your skin needs treatment, NOT foundation! So, don't try to disguise unhealthy skin; see a skin specialist!

Remember to wear an SPF cream every time you go out!

The skin damage produced by the sun is irreversible and is the primary cause of ageing, so look after your skin. You don't need to tan until you become brown. A sun-kissed look is attractive, but a sunburnt look is very unattractive, and everyone knows the harmful effects of long-term sun exposure.

Stay away from the sun most of the time. You only need very little time in the sun to get your daily vitamin D dosage.

Staying in the sun for too long without protection will cause sun spots, age spots and early wrinkles, especially on the face, neck and cleavage.

Ageing gracefully, without too many interventions, is terrific, but try to delay the ageing process for as long as possible.

You are lucky if you have naturally beautiful brown or black skin. But if you are pale and with great skin, you are just as fortunate, so love and protect your skin.

Refrain from extensive tanning because the cons of tanning overtake the pros.

Self-tanning products
Fake tanning should not exist at all! It's unattractive, it stinks, and, when poorly applied, it downgrades your look. You want to stand out in a crowd through your elegance, not vulgarity. You may get some attention, but there are better ways of attracting attention.
The orange look of fake tanning is not associated with refinement.

The smell
The ingredients and chemicals used in self-tanning lotion often vary, but the one responsible for the tanning effect has a particular smell. Beauty companies may tell you that their self-tanning products don't smell, but it's only marketing. That unpleasant odour may not be as potent in some tanning products, but it's always there!

The look
Applying self-tanning lotion is more complex than applying moisturiser. If you don't follow all the steps accurately, you are left with blotches, streaks or looking orange.

The mess

You must be very careful with applying it; the colour can transfer even after you wash the self-tanning lotion. Imagine wearing light colour clothes or sleeping on white sheets! I doubt a gentleman would be thrilled to see you again if you left his sheets stained after a night together.

Try to keep things in your beauty routine simple. The more natural you are, the easier it will be for you to keep yourself youthful and healthy.

Tanning beds are also a big no-no, as they are incredibly harmful. If you want to learn about the dangerous effects of bed tanning, research. And stop going to the salon to tan!

I cannot stress how important it is to keep a healthy routine when it comes to your skin.
Clean your face thoroughly before going to bed.
Keep your skin hydrated and moisturised.
Have regular facials and treat any breakouts correctly.
Clear skin is more important than makeup; you cannot hide unhealthy skin under layers of makeup because it shows in a good light.

So hiding is not a solution. Treating is the solution.

NOTES:
• Skin foundation is not always necessary
• Clean your skin daily before bed
• Wear SPF every time you go out during the day
• Protect your face when sunbathing
• Don't use fake tan
• Don't use sunbeds
• Keep your skin hydrated and moisturised
• Sleep on a silk pillowcase
• Have regular facials and treat breakouts correctly

~ 19 ~

ACNE

Acne is the most common skin condition, and many reasons can cause it, so the best thing is to find out what are the reasons that cause yours, rather than trying to hide it under layers of makeup because, that will never work. And while puberty acne usually clears up around the mid-twenties, some people are affected by this skin condition even later in adulthood.

Acne is not contagious, but the skin looks ill and unattractive during severe breakouts. And while it is true that cultural influences guide the perception of beauty, acne is considered unattractive in every culture, and a clear complexion is always seen as beautiful.

The good news is that you can treat this skin condition. Still, it's a long process, and you must be prepared to commit to the treatment for the whole period, as advised by your dermatologist, because stopping it too early will make the treatment inefficient.

The treatment may involve acne creams and sometimes, you must take antibiotics for several months to reduce the skin's bacteria and inflammation.

It is crucial to see a specialist who will determine the severity of your acne and prescribe a course of treatment customised to you.

They will offer skincare solutions, natural treatment options, and perhaps homemade skin remedies.

They will talk to you about the link between the gut and skin and advise what foods to introduce into your diet to help your skin.

The skin specialist will choose a skincare regime that must be kept every day and never neglected, no matter how tired or lazy you feel. You will be taught how to clean your face correctly, as soaps sometimes can disturb the Ph balance of your skin. Sometimes, cleansing creams may be recommended instead of soap.

Avoid skin toners containing alcohol; use toners with herbal extracts before moisturising.

In addition to a rigorous skincare regime and well-designed treatment plan, you may have to take some vitamin and mineral supplements. And, of course, if your diet is unhealthy, you must change it, if you want to start your transformation.

I know this may upset people, but I can tell you honestly that if you suffer from acne, you cannot jump this step, because no wealthy man will want to be with you long term if your skin is not healthy.

It's a reality you must know, so you are not surprised later.

Acne is a treatable skin condition, so find a specialist to deal with the problem. It is a significant step in your elevation, even if you are not necessarily looking to find someone.

NOTES
- See a dermatologist
- Don't try home remedies without getting advice from a specialist
- Keep a good skin routine
- Keep a healthy diet
- Keep hydrated
- Sleep well
- Don't touch your face when you are not cleansing it
- Use SPF when you are outside

~ 20 ~

NAILS

Your fingernails should be natural, tidy and short.

How short? Just to the fingertips or a few millimetres over the fingertips. Longer than that, they look vulgar.

The nail varnish should be neutral or very light colours. Also, clear varnish is always seen as classy and tidy, or if you wish to wear something bold, red is the best choice.

Most men do not find blue, black or other unusual nail polish colours attractive. But rich men, in particular, find them appalling.

Fake nails, especially the long ones (adorned with motifs, glitter and other embellishments), are tacky and downgrade your look.

How long should your toenails be?
The edge of your toenails should reach the tip of your toes. Any longer than that, they look unsanitary. On the other hand, cutting them too short can cause ingrown toenails.

Red toenails are seductive, but any discreet pedicure is attractive. It just needs to be impeccable! And an immaculate pedicure is not something you do only in the summer when you show your toes. A well-groomed pedicure is part of your hygiene, and your feet should be impeccable all year round.

Besides keeping your toenails in excellent condition all year round as part of good hygiene, there may be some occasions or events you will be invited to where removing your shoes is a cultural custom or etiquette. So keep your fingernails and toenails impeccable at all times!

The look you present to people is critical, because it's what a man sees before you do anything else: before you open your mouth and get a chance to show your character.

And if your look is not impeccable, you may not even have the opportunity to show a rich man your great personality because he will not be interested.

You may think that this is very superficial. It is what it is. You can take it or leave it. A rich man has many options, so if you want to make him interested in you, you must have the kind of look that will intrigue him.

To attract a classy, wealthy gentleman, you must have an impeccable image, intelligence and a pleasing personality.

Otherwise, other men may not be interested in these little details. But it is improbable that these men will be wealthy.
The choice is always yours!

And just as you want to feel free to choose your partner, rich men should be allowed to decide without being criticised for their preferences.

So, wealthy men don't like very long nails, unusual nail polish colours or untidy nails.

Keep your manicure and pedicure simple, natural and impeccable!

NOTES:
• Your fingernails should not be longer than 2-3 mm above the tip of your fingers
• Your toenails should not be longer than the tip of your toes
• Keep your nails red, nude, pastel pink or clear
• Do not use black nail varnish or any other unusual colours
• Do not glue glitter or other embellishments on your nails
• Do not use fake nails
• Your fingernails and toenails must be impeccable

WHY RICH MEN DON'T LIKE TO BE WITH FAKE-LOOKING WOMEN?

After covering all the physical aspects, I wanted to dedicate a chapter to why rich men don't like to be in a serious relationship with a woman who is fake looking.

Before I continue with this chapter, I need to remind you that this book is about **classy** wealthy men:

- aristocrats
- men who come from a wealthy background and are in a profession, a business, or an industry which made them even richer
- men who came from a modest background but were highly educated and had professions which made them very rich
- men who came from a modest background, and even though they weren't academically trained, they had very successful businesses and are now part of the high society

These are the main categories of men I studied for this book.

I know that many trendy nouveau rich don't mind women with plastic surgeries or wearing fake nails, hair extensions and heavy makeup. And it's okay. But this book is not about these men.

This book is about the traditional classy men with very high standards regarding themselves and the people they associate with. And I will explain why these men do not like to be in a serious relationship with a woman whose plastic surgeries or various beauty enhancements and procedures are too evident.

You may think, "But I've seen many women who had surgical procedures on their face and body accompanied by rich men". That's very true. There are many such situations, and I'll explain below the three most met scenarios of a rich man being with a woman who has had very obvious cosmetic procedures.

First scenario

Very often, a wealthy wife (who came or not from money) starts having cosmetic procedures during the marriage, but rarely beforehand.

She was likely natural and beautiful when she met her future rich husband, but she resorted to procedures to maintain her looks as she aged.

So next time you see a woman married to a rich guy, and it's clear that she's had a lot of work done, remember that it's very likely that she **first** married the guy and **then** underwent the cosmetic transformation. Not the other way around.

Plastic surgery is a relatively common practice among wealthy married women, even though it is rare that the husbands are happy with the wives' transformations. But one cannot easily walk away when one shares feelings, years of marriage, children, and social life.

The second scenario is when women with plastic surgeries were already wealthy when they married rich guys.

Those women started having cosmetic surgeries during the marriage or beforehand. But it doesn't matter. Being wealthy before marriage, the women in this category had much more than their physical appearance when the rich men settled for them: maybe a great intellect, an affluent background, inheritance, power - or perhaps, all of the above!

So, when a man meets a very accomplished woman, he can easily overlook some plastic surgeries. But, again, are the men happy with their wives' choices? Probably not, but other more important things keep them together.

If you don't have the wealth, but you have your looks, intelligence and personality, don't compromise any of them! Just as you seek high-calibre men, high-calibre men have high standards regarding women.

The third scenario when you see wealthy men with women who've had work done is when the rich man is married, and perhaps his marriage lacks physical intimacy; therefore, he finds comfort in the arms of another woman. In this case, the man is interested in things other than her artificial enhancements.

If the man is in an unhappy marriage, he may even feel that he is starting to have feelings for the "other" woman. But, of course, it's only physical.

Most of the time, the man realises it's a mistake and decides to save his marriage and leave the mistress.

Very rarely, the married man in an affair gets divorced and keeps the mistress.

This last scenario is improper, and no classy woman will find herself in this situation as being "the other woman". So never date married men!

***

So, whenever you see married rich men accompanied by women with lots of cosmetic procedures, it is usually one of the three scenarios above.

But getting back to the title of this chapter, generally, wealthy men DON'T want to be with fake looking women!

Here are some answers from rich men, when I asked why they don't like fake looking women:

- They encounter many women through work and social life, and they have plenty of options, so why should they settle for someone who feels that needed work to be attractive, when they can date someone naturally beautiful?!

- When they go out with someone, it's not only how they feel about their companion, but it matters to them how their friends, family, business associates, etc., perceive them and their choices. If the woman on their arm looks fake and they need to attend a family or business gathering, someone may think (or perhaps even mention) that the woman has had a lot of plastic surgery. This situation would be something they would happily avoid.

- Asked about heavy makeup, the men said they dislike kissing a face covered in powders and foundations and hate getting "the stuff" on their suits. Every wealthy man I asked answered that they preferred women with less makeup.

- When they discover that the woman has extensions, they freak out at the thought of being left with the hair in their hand if they touch her head.

- They find fake eyelashes unattractive because it's evident they are not real, and they don't want an unpleasant surprise when the woman takes them off and may look completely different.

- They feel the same about women who colour their eyebrows with a pencil: unattractive and unnecessary.

- They are entirely against tattooed and microbladed eyebrows. From up close, it is visible that there is no hair where hair should be. Some said it's the same as if a man would tattoo a moustache or beard on his face, and when you are up close, you can see that there is no hair.

- Enhanced lips look fake most of the time. And the contrast is significant when the woman with enhanced lips sits or stands next to a woman with natural lips.

- Regarding large breasts (natural or cosmetically enhanced), classy men prefer women who can dress with taste and the breasts don't "overflow" from their clothes. So, if the woman is top-heavy, classy men like when she dresses so that her breasts don't become "the main attraction" at a social gathering.

- Long, fake nails are unattractive and unhygienic, and wealthy men prefer shorter well-groomed nails.

- They see excessive Botox or too many surgical interventions as underlying low self-esteem issues.

These opinions are of the rich men with class, who don't understand why women alter their appearances to such an extent.

If you want to attract a classy, wealthy man, stay away from hair extensions, tattooed eyebrows, microbladed eyebrows, long fake nails, excessive Botox, unnecessary surgical procedures and anything so evident that they would feel embarrassed with you in public.

However, other categories of wealthy men have different preferences and standards. So if the type of wealthy individual that attracts you is **not** the classy gentleman, ignore all the above and follow your heart!

***

I remember numerous instances when I saw women who seemed stunning, although it was evident that they had "work done". But when put next to other remarkable women (who were also natural and without cosmetic interventions), they stood out for all the wrong reasons.

Next to natural beauties, the cosmetically-enhanced women didn't look so beautiful anymore. Every time I saw that contrast, I realised why classy, rich men prefer naturally looking women, with subtle makeup and a feminine demeanour.

Many wives of rich men indeed have plastic surgeries, but cosmetic interventions often start during the marriage. And although most husbands are not thrilled when the wife goes down that route, some may understand that she may be going through a crisis, she may not feel as attractive as before, and she may be trying to maintain her youth.

By that point, other things are keeping them together: feelings, perhaps children, and of course, the fact that his wife is free to do as she wishes with her body and even if he may not like it, there is not much he can do about it.

Everyone should feel free to do with their body as they wish.

The advice given here should **only** be considered by women who want to meet a wealthy guy and appeal to him.

I studied rich men for over two decades and am relaying their likes and dislikes here.

If your goal is **not** to attract a wealthy gentleman, you can have as many surgeries as you wish and wear as many fake eyelashes and nails as you want, because there are men out there who will not be bothered by any of these. Of course, it's unlikely that these men will be wealthy and classy, but there will always be men for every type of woman!

And just as it is your choice to decide what man you like, it is the men's choice to like what they want.

At the beginning of this chapter, I mentioned how effortless it is for the rich to find women with natural beauty, which is why they rarely compromise when they meet someone new.

In conclusion, rich men prefer women who preserve their beauty through proper hygiene and a healthy lifestyle.

And my advice to women who consider plastic surgeries is that, even if you marry a rich man and feel you want to fight the ageing process, find gentler ways to do it. Or, if you have plastic surgeries later in life, don't exaggerate. It reeks of insecurity.

There are very few situations when something needs repair, and it's usually to do with a nose which is too large for one's face, crooked teeth, or maybe some problem with which one was born or following an accident.

Otherwise, keep your looks as natural as you can!

And always remember that wealthy individuals want the woman by their side to be beautiful, intelligent, **and kind**! They greatly respect and appreciate gentle and compassionate women, so be careful what you work on during your elevating process. Work on your interior as well, not only on your exterior.

No matter the age, kindness will always be sexy!

22

If you want to elevate yourself and enter high society, NEVER HAVE AFFAIRS WITH MARRIED MEN OR MEN IN A RELATIONSHIP!

It's essential to understand why you should NEVER flirt or respond to the flirty advances of a married man.

It doesn't matter what he tells you.

It's not honourable to embark on such an affair, even if you like the man. And if you were foolish enough to let it happen, the situation becomes very complicated as soon as feelings develop.

A rich man will undoubtedly dump his mistress if a divorce costs him most of his wealth (which can happen if the wife hires a good divorce lawyer). Therefore, almost always, a rich man will choose his wealth over his mistress.

And you will be left with the stigma of "that woman who had an affair with a married man", an act which will haunt you for a long time. And I'm not talking about the guilt (because I don't believe you feel too much guilt; otherwise, you wouldn't have let it happen).

I mean the networking, which will be much more challenging for you once people brand you a "homewrecker".

You will find that most wealthy individuals (from a certain level up, on the social ladder) know each other. Therefore, if you had a relationship with a wealthy married man, it is likely that, while attending future events, you might be recognised by someone who found out about the unfortunate affair.

The men in that social circle will probably be more forgiving, but the women with whom you will come in contact, from then on, will exclude you from their group.

And you must understand that other women's input is valuable in elevating yourself and climbing the social ladder.

It's imperative to keep the women of influence on your side. Because if they like you, they invite you to exclusive events and dinner parties and introduce you to their single male friends and relatives.

But if they hear from someone that, sometime in the past, you went out with someone's husband, they will be very unforgiving and some, even spiteful. So you would become a social pariah.

Therefore, never respond to a man's flirtation advantages if he's not single, no matter how much you think you like him. You train your mind not to like unavailable men! If they are married, it doesn't matter how attractive they are and how many other qualities they have! YOU WALK AWAY!

Being elegant requires a complete transformation: the way you look, talk, walk, think, and behave must be at very high standards. And respect and high morals are crucial in your transformation.

As I've mentioned, keep your reputation intact; otherwise, your elevating process will be much more challenging!

~ 23 ~

STUDY YOUR BODY

Before you start creating your capsule wardrobe, you must determine these essential things:
- your body shape

- your top size
- your bottom size
- your bra size
- your shoe size
- the colours which suit you

~ 24 ~

BODY SHAPES

Learn to dress for your body shape and to enhance your best features.
The hourglass is the most feminine shape, that most women strive for.

If you **are** an hourglass, that's the shape you want your clothes to show.
If you **are not** an hourglass, that's the shape you want your clothes to create.

The main female body shapes:

Hourglass
- their shoulders and hips have the same measurements
- their waist is well-defined, and it's the smallest part of their body
- bust can range from small to large (depending on the whole body frame)

Athletic (or rectangle)
- their body looks like a column
- they are not particularly curvy
- their shoulders and hips measurements are almost the same
- their waist is not well-defined
- they have a flat tummy
- they have slender legs

Pear (or triangle)
- they have narrow shoulders
- they have wider hips and a generous bottom
- they need a bigger size for the lower part of the body than the upper part

Inverted triangle
- their shoulders are the widest part of the body
- they have very little to no waist definition
- they have narrow hips
- they have slim, athletic legs
- their bust can range from small to large
- they need a bigger size for the upper part of the body than the lower part

Apple shape
- they have an average to a larger bust
- they have narrow hips

- their waist is not well defined
- they carry weight around the midsection
- they have slimmer legs

The five body shapes mentioned above are the main shapes of women's bodies, but there are variants. You need to measure your shoulders, bust, waist and hips; write down the measurements and check the information against different online publications to determine your correct body shape.

After determining your body shape, research and find the types of clothes that flatter your figure.

Knowing your correct body shape, you will learn to accentuate certain parts, hide others, create a waist if the waist is not well defined, and elongate, balance and harmonise your features, to align your body beautifully.

Remember that you should dress not only for your shape but for your age too. So, if you are a 20-year-old woman, you can be a little more daring than you would be if you are a conservative 60-year-old woman. But if you are a mature woman, a more reserved way of dressing would be appropriate.

COLOURS

Study what colours you can wear to suit your skin tone and hair colour. Then, create a customised colour palette.

There are websites and apps which can help you with that. So do your homework and find out what suits you, because sometimes you may like a colour, but the colour may not like you. Do in-depth research to find the shades that work for you, and you will never have to shop from the wrong colour section again.

It doesn't mean that if you find out that a specific colour doesn't suit you, you will never be able to wear it again. You can always wear that colour on the lower part of your body so it doesn't interfere with your complexion. And you can choose a colour for your upper part that complements your skin and hair and matches well with the tone of the garment on your lower body.

Sometimes it's a matter of undertone, and choosing the right undertone of the same colour will make your outfits look better on you.

So after the colour test, you may find out that (let's say) purple doesn't suit you. It could be that only certain shades don't work for you. There are many shades of purple in two categories: warm purple and cool purple, and you have to choose the right shade. The same goes for any colour.

Most colours have a **mass tone** (the colour you see immediately) and an **undertone** (a less noticeable colour).

Spend time studying and understanding colours, find the colours that suit you and create your personalised colour palette.

***

If you start your transformation in spring or autumn, get two trench coats (one in a light colour and one in a darker colour, depending on your complexion). Make sure the coats fit you well, and if you are smaller in stature, opt for a shorter trench that finishes just above the knees. If necessary, take it to a tailor for a perfect fit.

After you know which colours suit you:

1) Use layers of pastel-coloured clothing in **spring** for fresh, feminine, and elegant looks.

Create your spring palette from pastel colours such as lilac, mint, baby blue, mellow rose, white, beige, vanilla, light aqua, buttercup etc.

2) In **autumn**, layer with more neutral shades of tan, beige, chocolate, sand, warm grey, navy, sage green, oyster white, golden, or silver accents etc. Again, find the colours to suit the complexion of your skin and your hair, as you cannot wear any random colour. Choosing clothes in the wrong colours can make you look washout or unhealthy, so use the colours from your customised palette, so you glow every season.

3) If you start your transformation in **winter**, choose your coats carefully. If your starting budget is limited, you must be wise about shopping for winter coats, as they are some of the most expensive items.

Your first coat should not be patterned or white. Instead, your winter coat should be a shade you can wear with various outfits and bags and add numerous scarves and shawls to create different looks.

If your coat is patterned, the looks you can create are limited.
If your coat is white, you risk staining it easily.

Ideally, start your winter wardrobe with at least two coats to alternate during the cold season - one of a lighter colour and one of a darker colour. You can purchase, for example, one beige, cream or light grey and one black or navy blue (depending on your complexion).

4) If it's **summer** when you decide to start your transformation, get some light-coloured linen clothes (shirts, trousers, skirts, and dresses), silk camisoles in various colours, and colourful scarves.

During the summer, experiment with some bright colours (as long as they are not neon), and when your budget allows, buy a couple of brilliant white dresses, too, since you'll probably have a little tan, which looks lovely in white.

And get many scarves: oversized and neck scarves (or neckerchiefs), in bright colours, pastel colours, patterned (Hermes style), pashminas, etc. The scarves are splashes of colours and patterns that can brighten up simple outfits while preserving elegance.

They are versatile statement pieces; you can find them in various materials for every season.

And as usual, look for quality, not necessarily for the label. You can find beautiful scarves made of premium fabrics from unknown producers or little market stalls. Don't stretch your budget in order to buy designer items. If the quality is high, the brand's name is unimportant.

Buy less and buy quality!

~ 26 ~

MATERIALS

Choose clothes made of silk, cotton, linen, hemp, cashmere (and other types of wool) and even viscose.

Avoid polyester as much as you can. Polyester is a type of plastic which is cheap and harmful to your skin and the environment.

Natural fibres are more expensive, but you must start thinking differently about what you buy. Having a mindset for purchases which will be in your wardrobe for some years will make you look for higher quality and durability.

Let's say you start your transformation now. First, get what you need for the current season; ensure you have the right outfits for any upcoming events you may have signed up for. And for the rest of the items, shop gradually. You only need part of the capsule wardrobe at a time. Therefore, you can wait to buy everything in stages for each season.

The more expensive materials require better care and some crease with ease, which is why you should invest in a handheld steamer and use it daily, even for your pyjamas, loungewear, and house clothes.

Instead of wearing them with creases, steam them for a few minutes, and you will look and feel better. Remember that you aim to become elegant, so behave and look stylish always, even when no one sees you.

Creases on silk or linen after the garments have been steamed are acceptable. One can see the difference, so don't fret about this aspect!

But remember that a silk skirt creased after sitting down looks different from a silk skirt that has never been steamed in the first place. So, don't jump this step thinking that "the skirt will crease anyway, so what's the point in wasting time to steam/iron it"? Don't cut corners where you shouldn't!

Wear natural fibres because they are better for you and the environment. If you are careful with what you put **inside** your body, you should be just as thoughtful with what you put **on** your body.

Buy less and buy natural!

~ 27 ~

CLOTHES

They say that if you want to close a million-dollar deal, you must look like a million dollars!

Elevating your looks will increase your confidence levels, and you will begin attracting many exciting new people.

Start with clearing your wardrobe of anything cheap and tacky. Then, get rid of all the items that have holes, or look too worn, give to charity what you think you cannot sell, and put the rest on selling platforms: sell them as one lot or piece by piece.

But remember to abide by the terms and conditions of selling platforms. So if a person pays you for an item, you must post the item to the buyer within a few days. Because an elegant woman is trustworthy and respects everybody with whom she interacts.

Keep what looks and feels good and can be saved. Immediately throwing all your clothes away may not be the smartest thing.

For example, if you have an office job and wear mainly suits to work (or skirts & shirts or trousers & shirts), don't throw them all away when you start your capsule wardrobe, but do get rid of the ones that don't look good.

If your work clothes look cheap and boring, find a way to spruce them up. Take them to a good dry cleaner and ask them to remove any stains, repair pockets and the lining, change buttons, if needed, etc. Then, carry yourself confidently, and wear a simple, sleek bag, natural make-up, and impeccable hair and nails, which will elevate your appearance considerably.

After getting rid of probably two-thirds of your clothes, make a list with everything you need to create a capsule wardrobe. The following chapters will help with your list. If you can't save many pieces from your old wardrobe, the list will probably be long, but you don't need to buy everything at once.

From now on, you will learn to "shop smart".

~ 28 ~

UNDERWEAR

Before buying any bras, arrange an appointment with a specialist to be fitted for a bra. You will be surprised, but many women have been wearing the wrong bra for years because they've never had a bra fitting to determine their correct size.

Not to mention that your bra size may differ slightly, depending on the brand, so to be sure that you wear the correct bra, have a bra fitting every six months to a year.

An ill-fitted bra is uncomfortable and makes your clothes fall badly on you, so see a specialist, get a fitting, and buy a few sets of bras in different colours. You can start with white, black and your skin colour, to ensure that you have enough to wear underneath almost any item of clothing.

It's essential to get underwear in YOUR skin tone because if you are dark-skinned and wear a light shade of nude, your underwear will show through your garments. Just as if you are light-skinned and wear a darker nude shade, the underwear will be visible underneath white clothes.

Make sure you determine your correct size and skin colour tone to buy the right underwear, as your body needs prepping before you put your clothes on, for the outfits to look fabulous while wearing them.

Always remember:
The bra is too small if the breasts spill out and are not enclosed in the cups.
The bra is too big if the cup is loose.

The band underneath the cups (which wraps around your torso) should form a straight

line. The band is responsible for most of the support.
The shoulder straps keep the bra in place, not lift or offer support.

There are over 40 types of bras, but you only need some of them. So, the essential bras and the three colours you need are:

- t-shirt bras for comfortable everyday use (your skin colour, white and black)
- sports bras for physical exercise (in your skin colour, white and black)
- strapless bras and multi-way bras for Bardot, strapless or halterneck tops and dresses (in your skin colour, white and black)
- full cup stick-on bras for backless dresses (in your skin colour, white and black); never get silicone stick-on bras - they are not classy
- for large-chested women, balconette bras for support (in your skin colour, white and black)

Please note that the above types of bras are what a woman needs in her wardrobe to cover and support her chest in most outfits.

But there are many other types you can research and try when you are curious to learn more.

I didn't include bras for erotic endeavours because sexy lingerie is very personal, and everyone should wear what makes them feel sexy.

The ones on the list above are the essential bras you must own for all the outfits to look good on you. And it would help if you had them in those three colours: your skin colour, white and black. However, if it's too big an expense for you to get them in the three colours, get one of each type from the list above in your skin colour.

Bras in your skin tone are more important than in other colours. So, don't buy things you don't need. Instead, start building your wardrobe with what is essential.

Throw away any underwear items with holes or threads hanging or that are too worn, faded, or do not fit properly.

Get your knickers to match the bras, and never wear big ugly knickers, even if no one sees you. When you feel good in your clothes, smell good, and your skin, teeth, hair and nails are fabulous, your confidence levels will increase.

And there is nothing sexier than a confident, feminine woman who knows her worth.

So while for bras, you must be fitted by a specialist to ensure that you wear the right size, the knickers which fit you well are, generally, the same size as for all the garments on the lower side of your body (trousers, skirts).

Same as with the bras, get whatever sexy knickers you want when you are intimate with your partner, but also purchase enough pairs of seamless knickers in your skin colour for the more delicate garments.

Nude underwear underneath any colour garments is optional.
But underneath white (or light-coloured) clothes, it's COMPULSORY!

Never wear a white bra underneath a white (or light-coloured) shirt/t-shirt/dress!
Likewise, never wear white knickers underneath white (or light-coloured) trousers or skirts!

The white underneath white becomes even brighter, making your underwear visible through the garments. And that is not elegant!

When wearing white, ensure your underwear is not only your skin colour but also seamless, as lines poking through fine material are unsightly.

NOTES:
- Get fitted for a bra
- Determine your correct skin colour (your shade of nude)
- Your essential bras are:
  - t-shirt bra
  - sports bra
  - strapless bra
  - multi-way bra
  - full cup stick-on bra
  - balconette bra (for a large bust)
- If you can only start with one colour, get them in your shade of nude
- Purchase enough pairs of seamless knickers in your shade of nude
- Have sexy lingerie for fun times with your partner

TOPS, BLOUSES, SHIRTS

Choose your tops, blouses, and shirts mainly in light and pastel colours (from the palette designed for your skin tone). Also, get some bold colours to brighten a dark suit, trousers, or skirt.

As with every item of clothing, knowing your body shape will help you choose correctly.

For example, pear shapes (triangles) can wear padded tops or tops with puffy sleeves, horizontal stripes etc. In contrast, inverted triangles should avoid those tops.

That is why, before purchasing anything, measure yourself and determine your body shape and size.

Stay away from busy patterns, and never wear tops with text, someone's face, stickers, glitter or other embellishments.
They look childish or tacky.

T-shirts are not elegant.

Choose something more sophisticated when you don't exercise, even to wear around the house.
T-shirts, leggings and sportswear worn outside your gym will not help elevate your look.

Because there are many types and models of blouses, tops and shirts, research and choose what suits your body shape. For example, some have pussybows, some have appliques, others are asymmetric, or maybe have a sweetheart neckline or a boat neckline etc. So, learn what suits your body type and colour complexion.

Be mindful of the colours you choose for your tops, to combine well them with the trousers and the skirts in your wardrobe. At the beginning of your transformation, versatility is essential, because buying mainly separates allows you to combine them and create many outfits. And you can give personality to a neutral outfit just by adding accessories.

For example, if you have in your capsule wardrobe an **ivory silk shirt**, these are some of the different occasions when you can wear it beautifully:

- Wear your ivory silk shirt with an ivory or cream skirt, and add a tan-colour belt and a scarf in bold colours **for an elegant lunch**.

- You create another fabulous outfit **for a smart casual dinner** with the same ivory silk shirt, a pair of navy-tailored trousers, and a long string of pearls (even faux pearls, as a statement piece).
- Or you can wear an ivory-coloured camisole underneath your ivory silk shirt, roll up its sleeves, leave 3-4 buttons open and tuck the shirt into a pair of jeans **for a casual look**.
- You can wear the same ivory silk shirt underneath a dark-coloured structured dress **for a corporate meeting**.
- Or you can wear your ivory silk shirt over a long summer dress tied at the waist **for a relaxed evening stroll**.

Here, you have five occasions when you can wear your shirt combined with other pieces, and I can assure you that, if done correctly, you will look fabulous!

And you can make countless other outfits with this garment, so choose your separates wisely when creating your capsule wardrobe.

Essential tops, blouses, and shirts for a capsule wardrobe:

- one crisp white long-sleeve fitted shirt made from high-quality cotton
- one crisp blue long-sleeve fitted shirt made from high-quality cotton
- one white oversized linen shirt (to wear over camisoles and summer dresses)
- one off-white, ivory or cream-coloured silk blouse (for your body shape) to create sophisticated day-time outfits
- one navy, red or other dark colour silk blouse (for your body shape) to create sophisticated evening outfits
- few pastel-coloured tops and blouses to combine with your trousers and skirts
- light fabric camisoles in various colours
- fine cashmere or merino wool turtlenecks in white, black and nude (for pairing them up with other separates to instantly elevate an outfit in every season)
- cashmere and wool jumpers and sweaters, in dark and light colours, for the colder months

When purchasing clothes for the colder seasons, remember that getting a good quality sweater from warm but fine fabric will allow you to wear it underneath a blazer or a coat in winter and by itself in autumn or spring.

So opting for a sweater from a finer blend rather than a thick oversized jumper will be versatile, and you can enjoy it more often.

Always shop smart and think of the price per wear!

~ 30 ~

TROUSERS & JEANS

When you build your capsule wardrobe, shop for trousers in materials suitable for the current season.

For example:
- If you start your transformation in the summer, look for light, breathable materials and prioritise summer trousers.
- If you start your transformation in the winter, shop first for structured, tailored trousers which are thicker and retain heat.

Buying winter trousers in the middle of the summer or summer trousers in the winter would be a good tip when your capsule wardrobe is complete (as you may find sale items at the end of a season). But when you start building your wardrobe, you should budget carefully.

Pay attention to the length of the trousers you choose. Go for trousers and jeans which elongate your legs, not for ones which make your legs look short.

When you try something on, use a full-length mirror and check how your body is segmented: your upper part should look shorter than the lower part. Therefore, always choose trousers which elongate your legs.

You can't control how your body is constructed, but you can control how you dress to create pleasing proportions: shorter upper part and longer lower part.

Also, take into consideration that skinny jeans don't fit everyone!

You can be a slim woman, but skinny jeans will not suit you if you have thick calves. Skinny jeans look good only on women with thin thighs and thin calves. The height doesn't matter!

So, just because you are tall and thin doesn't necessarily mean you will look good wearing skinny jeans. If your legs are not evenly slim, and you may have thicker calves, choose a different cut to suit you.

Shop for your body shape and choose only trousers and jeans to suit your body!

The most elegant trousers and jeans are:
- tailored trousers
- classic pleated trousers
- narrow leg trousers
- wide leg trousers
- straight leg trousers
- cigarette trousers
- palazzo trousers
- high-waisted trousers
- bootcut jeans
- straight jeans
- slim jeans
- skinny jeans (**only** if your legs are slender and your calves are thin)

But first of all, determine your body shape, and only afterwards, choose from the list above what suits you.

Do not choose the following types: harem, sweatpants, hot pants, baggy jeans, and ripped jeans! They are not elegant, and they downgrade your look.

Don't wear leggings unless you are exercising; never wear flesh-coloured or see-through leggings for any reason! **Leggings and yoga pants are for sport only and should not be worn as part of a casual outfit.**

You should build your wardrobe slowly and mindfully, considering the garment pieces you need first. Never be impulsive with your purchases! You want to create a capsule wardrobe which is versatile and timeless. Stay away from trends and start with trousers and jeans in colours which are easy to combine: black, navy, grey, white, beige, and cream.

~ 31 ~

SKIRTS

Because there are so many types of skirts, based on length and structure, first, you must determine which types of structure and length suit your body shape.

For example, if you are a pear shape, don't choose a skirt with extra material on the hip area (like peplum skirts), as it will make you look bigger. The same applies to patterned or bold colour skirts, which may not help a pear shape.

However, skirts with extra material on the hips, patterned skirts, and skirts with detailing or in bold colours will suit an inverted triangle by adding volume on the lower part and creating the illusion of an hourglass.

Research and find the suitable types of skirts to suit your body shape, and get a few pieces you can combine with tops and shirts from your capsule wardrobe.

As with every item of your clothing, when building your elegant capsule wardrobe, avoid patterned skirts, bold and statement skirts. Otherwise, the number of combinations you can create with such skirts is limited.

For example, a multicoloured, heavy-patterned tafetta skirt may be fabulous for a special event. But you cannot wear such a noticeable item in other combinations and for different occasions.

So, keep the statement pieces for later, when your capsule wardrobe is complete.

For now, buy your separates mainly in neutral colours, choose various lengths to show off your best features, and have fun accessorising them to create different looks.

So, after deciding the structure and length that flatter your body shape, **choose from the following types, but only the ones that suit you:**

- pencil
- pleated
- straight
- A-line
- layered
- asymmetrical
- draped
- wrap

Again, please note that maybe **only** some of the above skirt types suit your body shape, so research before purchasing clothes. You want to create a versatile wardrobe covering most of the events in your life.

There are many other types of skirts if you want to experiment, but the list I made here shows the types that are easy to combine with tops, to create elegant looks.

32

DRESSES

By now, you should know your body shape, the correct dress size and what suits you. So, stick with the rules you learned about your body shape, shop smart and only buy simple and versatile dresses.

You should experiment with bolder items once your capsule wardrobe is complete.

For example, when you are at the beginning of your transformation, it is unlikely that you will need to attend a white-tie or a black-tie event immediately, so you don't need to shop (just yet) for a floor-length gown or an evening dress.

Ideally, you would shop for versatile dresses that are casual enough to wear during the day and smart enough that, with the right accessories, you can turn them into suitable outfits for informal dinners.

A good example of a simple and versatile dress is a sheath or pencil dress:
- it can be worn with a fitted blazer at the office
- remove the blazer, add a patterned scarf and some bangles and you can wear it for an informal lunch with a friend
- you can add a hat and a clutch and wear the same dress at a more formal daytime event, like a christening or at the races
- add a large semiprecious stone neckless, or a small diamond pendant, or a long string of pearls, or a dressier cape, and you can wear the same dress in the evening

This is why it's important to think (before you buy) about the different ways you can wear your capsule wardrobe items.

Finding elegant dresses is relatively easy when your figure is between UK size 8 and UK size 12 (or 6 if you are petite). So, lose the extra weight before you start shopping to create your capsule wardrobe.

Always go for the classy and timeless cuts rather than following trends. Look only for classic pieces you think you can wear in 10, 20, or 30 years and still look elegant. Of course, it doesn't necessarily mean that you will be wearing these clothes in 10, 20, or 30 years, but it serves as guidance on how to build your wardrobe with classy looks.

The most elegant and versatile colours are white, black, navy, grey, tan, cream, ivory, champagne, beige and all the pastel colours.

An essential fact about dresses is that informal dinners happen much more often than formal dinners. Therefore, you must first purchase dresses you are more likely to need.

When you are at the beginning of your journey and must budget carefully, I advise you NOT to buy, but to hire dresses for formal events, especially for the ones where the dress needs to be spectacular (for black or white tie functions).

Don't buy dresses for formal events if your capsule wardrobe is incomplete!

Buying a cheap floor-length gown would downgrade your appearance. And on the other hand, purchasing something too expensive will be a bad investment, because it may take some time before you wear it again. So, for a while, don't splash on formal evening wear! Instead, hire when you need and keep your money for the more versatile pieces.

The essential dresses that an elegant woman needs are:

- pencil dress (or sheath dress) in a dark colour (preferably black or navy blue) to create various outfits for informal events and activities, both day and evening
- pencil dress (or sheath dress) in a light colour (beige, cream, off-white, ivory, champagne) to create various outfits mainly for daytime wear
- knee-length cocktail dress (preferably in a darker colour and of a flowy material) for dates and informal evening events
- pastel-coloured summer dress (above the knee, knee-length or midi) for everyday use in the summer
- maxi beach dress (white or in a light colour) for picnics or holidays in the sun
- smart casual long-sleeve dress in a thicker fabric to wear on colder days

Try the dresses on as they are, then add jackets, cardigans, scarves, pearls, capes or shawls, belts, hats etc.

Spend some time and put together various outfits with your capsule wardrobe dresses; use Pinterest or other platforms for inspiration, take photos and save them in a folder on your phone.

The ones on the list above are all the dresses you need in your capsule wardrobe.

Choose the colours wisely:
- Stay away from heavy patterns or bold colours. Neutral tones make your dresses versatile, and you can create tens of outfits just by layering and accessorising.

Choose the materials wisely:
- Elegant pencil dresses are structured and made of viscose or wool. They shouldn't feel and look flimsy. They shouldn't be ribbed, too tight or made of jersey, light cotton, lace or any thin fabric.
- The cocktail dress should be of a soft and flowy material, such as chiffon or silk satin. A stiff and structured dress on a date or cocktail party is not the best look.
- The ideal summer dress would be made of linen or linen blend. Linen has a luxurious feel and look, even if it creases easily. A certain amount of creases is accepted on linen.

- A maxi beach dress made out of superior cotton fabric can look fabulous.
- An elegant long sleeve dress for cold weather should be made of merino wool, cashmere, viscose or thick silk fabric.

You don't need to buy formal attire at the beginning of your transformation because formal dresses are not versatile. Therefore, they are a bad investment. Instead, rent any formal wear when you need to attend a formal event.

NOTES:
- Capsule wardrobe dresses:
  - ✓ pencil dress (or sheath dress) dark colour
  - ✓ pencil dress (or sheath dress) light colour
  - ✓ cocktail dress
  - ✓ summer dress
  - ✓ maxi dress
  - ✓ winter dress
- Choose colours wisely
- Choose materials wisely
- Create outfits and save them to a folder on your phone

33

BLAZERS & JACKETS

Even though you don't need to buy designer clothes to build an elegant wardrobe, I recommend looking for quality.

Purchasing a beautiful designer piece may be a good investment in the long term. But if your budget doesn't allow you to purchase it with ease, then it's unwise to do so.

If you take your time to search, you can find good quality clothes from lesser-known brands to last you a long time.

However, while finding a good quality summer dress at a market stall while on holiday may be possible, it is different with blazers and jackets. Unfortunately, you can't find well-fitted blazers everywhere. And this is why you should purchase your blazers and jackets only from specialised brands. Otherwise, cheap versions can downgrade your look.

Blazers and jackets take incredible skill to be created well, and high-quality blazers and jackets can be worn for many years and even be passed on to the next generations.

So, when you start shopping for outerwear, buy gradually and consciously. You shouldn't rush to spend your monthly budget on a couple of blazers. But you shouldn't opt for the cheapest option from budget stores, either! Instead, wait and purchase the right ones.

Everyone should have in their wardrobe:
- A fitted black or navy blue blazer (single or double-breasted, depending on your body shape)
- A tweed fitted blazer in a slightly lighter colour, such as dark olive or tawny
- A linen blazer in a light colour such as ivory, off-white or a pastel colour (while the first two blazers look best fitted, you should get the linen blazer one size up for a more relaxed yet elegant summer look)
- A quilted or wax jacket in a dark colour such as black, navy blue, brown, dark grey or dark green

I cannot stress enough the importance of having these items in your wardrobe, as you will be invited to specific events and must dress appropriately.

You can wear the two fitted blazers mentioned above for a smart casual look, or you can wear them for dressier attire with the right accessories.

The oversized linen blazer is a must in the summer, especially on cooler evenings. Roll up or ruche its sleeves and it will instantly elevate a relaxed look.

The quilted or wax jacket can be great for travelling and outdoor activities, especially in the countryside.

And as with all other garments, before purchasing blazers and jackets, pay attention to your body shape, size and colour palette.

~ **34** ~

COATS

When buying large items like winter coats, avoid busy prints and patterns.

A heavily patterned winter coat is rarely elegant. And when you are at the beginning of your transformation, and your budget is limited, a garment like that wouldn't be a good investment, as it stands out, and you can't wear it as often as you would a classy coat.

From now on, whenever you buy clothes, you must consider the price per wear.

A winter coat with large prints or bold colours would be very noticeable, and you don't want to be seen wearing the same thing throughout winter.

If you can only buy two winter coats at the beginning, get two long tailored coats in two colours: one black and one lighter (beige, off-white, cream etc.), as they look timeless and are easy to accessorise. Don't buy oversized coats because they hide your figure, making you look frumpy.

Apart from the winter coat, another essential coat for your capsule wardrobe is a trenchcoat, which you can wear in spring and autumn and sometimes even in the colder days of summer or warmer days of winter.

A trenchcoat is classic and timeless and elevates your look instantly. And if you can afford, buy the trench in two colours (dark and light), the same as the winter coats.

The difference between coats (winter coats and trenchcoats) and blazers is that, sometimes, you may find good coats and trenchcoats in inexpensive high-street stores. However, one should purchase from a good tailoring brand when shopping for blazers.

Accessorising allows you to create loads of looks with your winter and trench coats.

You can wear them with the following:
- various hats
- different colour belts
- silk scarves
- oversized scarves, stoles and shawls worn in different styles:
  - ✓ around the neck
  - ✓ with different loops: single loop, double loop, triple loop, infinity loop
  - ✓ wrapped around shoulders
  - ✓ draped on your front
  - ✓ draped on your front and tied with the belt
  - ✓ draped on one side of the body (back and front) and tied with the belt
  - ✓ etc.

Search the Internet for ways to wear scarves, stoles and shawls and have fun styling your coats to create various looks.

~ 35 ~

ACCESSORIES

Achieving an elegant look takes as little as putting together a few pieces of clothing of the same colour and accessorising them with a scarf, glasses, hat, bag, or a beautiful piece of jewellery.

Visit antique markets, invest in a beautiful set of pearls (earrings and necklace or earrings and pendant), and don't listen to anyone who says that pearls are boring and old-fashioned. On the contrary, pearls are classy, elegant and timeless. And wearing pearls with almost any outfit can elevate your look instantly.

In terms of other pieces of jewellery to have at the beginning of your transformation, purchase a subtle pendant and studs in white gold (with or without semiprecious gems) and perhaps something similar in yellow gold. But, again, buy delicate pieces, nothing big and flashy.

Jewellery should be small and subtle, and the pieces you wear should complement your look, not overwhelm it.

If you cannot invest in a diamond pendant and studs (or other precious stones, such as ruby, sapphire or emerald), find a semiprecious stone pendant which is discreet and elegant.

Remember that wearing cheap large pieces of jewellery will make you seem flashy and may downgrade your look. No one will believe that the large necklace covering half your chest and the sparkly tiara are diamonds, unless you are royalty.

However, wearing a small pendant and studs will make you look classy, and you will get many admiring looks (and probably compliments) for your tasteful choice.

So, if your budget is limited and you are at the beginning of your transformation, get the following pieces of jewellery, as they are the easiest to wear with multiple outfits:
- **a set of pearls** (neckless and earrings or pendant and earrings)
- **two delicate sets of gold pendants and studs** (one in white gold and one in yellow gold, preferably; but if

you can only afford one set, opt for white gold as it's classier)

- **a subtle, precious stone pendant and earrings** (or a set with a semiprecious stone, if diamonds or other precious stones are too much over your budget)

Those four jewellery sets are enough. Any other pieces of jewellery would be lovely, but are not essential. Not for now. Remember that, for now, you must shop smart!

Later, when your capsule wardrobe is complete, you can purchase a few bold jewellery pieces for various occasions, but such investments are unnecessary at the beginning of your transformation.

When you can, invest in a couple of luxury scarves. They don't have to be from current collections. Instead, check outlets where you can find scarves from past collections. Classy items are timeless.

The idea is not necessarily to buy all your clothes from well-known designers, but to get a few pieces of high impact. For example, a Hermes scarf is exquisite and will add a touch of class, making you look sophisticated. And you can wear a Hermes scarf with the most basic, simple dress and look like a million dollars.

However, I cannot stress how important it is to say NO to buying fake or stolen goods! You encourage criminal operations, and an elegant woman doesn't do that!

Other accessories for your capsule wardrobe are:

- **elegant gloves in a few colours**
- **belts of various widths in black, caramel brown, nude and white**
- **scarves and hats in different colours**
- **sunglasses to suit the shape of your face**
- **tights in nude and black**

~ 36 ~

FOOTWEAR

When you start building your capsule wardrobe, choose a variety of shoes, sandals and boots in nude, brown, navy, black and maybe one in a bold colour, like red. Those colours will be easy to combine with various outfits.

Find shoes to suit your lifestyle and choose sleek and simple lines. Having some statement shoes is great, but they are unnecessary when you build your capsule wardrobe.

Educate yourself about the types of footwear (and heel size and models) so you know what you shop for.

Choose footwear and heel heights to give you comfort. High heels are feminine, but you must know how to walk in high heels gracefully. Record yourself walking and practice at home until you master the walk. And mastering the walk in high heels means more than just being able to stand or walk a few steps. You need to walk with grace and elegance and look very comfortable. So only leave the house in high heels IF you feel you can walk elegantly!

While stiletto high heels may make you look seductive, you must walk in them comfortably. Otherwise, you will look very clumsy. Also, it's important to remember that you don't want to look seductive always. There are occasions when a more demure look is required.

Stilettos can be elegant if worn with the right outfit. However, in other situations, they may look inappropriate. If you like stilettos, **wear the correct heel height and shoe type for each occasion**. For example, a pair of stiletto high-heel platform shoes are very inappropriate at a funeral. But a pair of pumps with a lower stiletto heel is elegant and suitable.

So, when choosing shoes for a capsule wardrobe, leave the very high heel shoes for later and first, look for pumps with different heels: high heels, mid-height heels and low heels (chunky or block heels).

At the start of building your wardrobe, pumps should be the primary type of shoes you look for. You can find them with soles, heels, toes and widths to suit any foot size. Then, all you have to do is try them on!

You should always try the shoes on before buying them! Or, if you are a fan of online shopping, **you should not keep the shoes if they don't fit properly**, just because it's too much hassle to return them! Always return ill-fitting shoes!

Also, be smart about buying your capsule wardrobe shoes. If you get shoes with simple, sleek lines, you can wear them as they are, or you can accessorise them with shoe clips, bows and scarves and turn them into entirely different shoes.

Search the internet, and you will find numerous blogs and vlogs showing how to dress up simple shoes with various accessories.

I suggest starting your shoe collection in colours which are easy to wear with any outfit: nude, brown, black, navy, grey etc. **Shoes in a nude** (your skin) **tone** are more important than black or other colours because **you can wear** them **with ANY COLOUR outfit!**

Despite what you may have heard, **black shoes are NOT the easiest to wear with any colour outfit.** There are many outfits for which black shoes are not suitable. **The nude colour is the easiest to pair.**

- If you must decide what colour your first pair of quality shoes should be, opt for nude (closest to your skin tone).
- If you have to decide what model, opt for pumps.
- If you have to decide on the heel size, opt for a mid-height heel (max 8.5cm)

Therefore, your first pair of high-quality shoes should be a pair of nude pumps

with mid-height heels (max 8.5cm)! Every woman should own this pair of shoes!

Now take some time to study:
- types of shoes
- types of sandals
- types of boots
- types of heels
- types of toes
- types of widths
- types of materials

Then you will get an idea of what footwear will suit your lifestyle and still be comfortable and elegant.

The essential footwear in your starting collection should be:
- several pairs of pumps with various size heels, from flat to high heels (in nude, brown, navy, black, grey and perhaps red)
- two pairs of sandals with mid-length or low heels (one nude and one white); because you may be walking more in summer
- one pair or two pairs of wedges and some pretty flip-flops (find flip-flops ornated with something like rhinestones or other stylish details; but in good taste, nothing over the top)

- one pair of simple, stylish sports shoes (in white or cream)
- one pair of knee-high boots with mid-height or lower heels (in a neutral colour)
- one pair of ankle boots with mid-height or lower heels (in a neutral colour)

Use the above list as a guide and purchase suitable footwear for your current season. For example, if you start your transformation in the middle of summer, you don't need to shop for knee-high boots. Instead, get only the essential shoes and find ways to style them to make them versatile.

Also, remember:
- Chunky trainers are not elegant. So instead, for your sporting activities, find a sleek pair of sports shoes, which will not make your foot look too big and don't have stickers, logos and tacky embellishments.
- Never wear sheepskin boots! They downgrade your look, and I am confident you can find something more attractive to keep your feet warm.
- Never wear your shoes dusty! Just before leaving the house, have another look and give them another wipe.

- If any heels or soles need repairing or replacing, have them done immediately.
- Make sure that you buy shoes which fit you properly. The sight of toes coming out of sandals and touching the pavement as you walk is an image that reeks of sloppiness.
- And although I covered this aspect in the "Nails" section, I'll mention it again: your pedicure must be immaculate every season, whether you wear sandals or not. But if you wear sandals and your toenails look filthy, then it is clear that you don't care enough about yourself and the people around you. An elegant woman won't subject anyone to such an appalling sight!

~ 37 ~

BAGS

When you buy bags, never go for the ones with large writing or patterns showing the brand from a mile away.

The bag doesn't even have to be a "designer bag". Nothing you wear **needs** to be designer for you to look elegant. You can get beautifully crafted bags which may not necessarily be by a well-known brand. Choose sleek designs and elegant colours which you can wear with various outfits.

Even with a large budget, you should be sensible about buying bags and other things.

But especially if your budget is limited, be wise about your spending, so be practical and only get essential bags.

If you are at the beginning of your journey and don't know if your current bags are elegant, or you want to buy new bags and are not sure about the colours or the models, use the following list as a guide for the items you need the most:
• a black structured tote bag
• a light-coloured (such as cream or beige) structured tote bag
• a crossbody (if you can only get one, go for black, dark grey or other dark colours; when you are comfortable purchasing your second crossbody, you can choose a lighter neutral colour)
• a day clutch (if you can only get one, go for nude or off-white)
• an evening clutch (a dark colour would be a good choice, or if you wish, you can go for something sparkly - but keep it classy!)

- a casual weekend bag
- a beach bag (canvas or straw)

These are the essentials. You don't need to get the whole list in one go but use it as guidance and notice that in terms of colours, I suggest black, dark grey, nude, cream, and beige. These colours make the bags more versatile; therefore, you don't need to spend too much and can use them with your whole wardrobe.

If the bags are structured, they look more elegant and sophisticated.

Floppy bags have a boho vibe and look more relaxed but less elegant.

So for your first purchases, always buy structured bags because they elevate your look.

Don't buy whimsical or quirky bags when you start building your wardrobe. If you want to purchase some statement bags, do it when you can afford to and only **after** buying all the essential pieces. But again, be sensible and think about the overconsumption and the environment!

And you don't have to break the bank to buy bags. You can find high-quality, fabulous bags at small manufacturers, craft fairs and museum gift shops, where independent artisans sell their handmade goods.

If a bag is beautiful, it doesn't need to be created by a well-known designer! Tie a silk scarf (or a Twilly) to its handle, and you make it look chic and sophisticated. But don't tie anything else to your bag besides a beautiful scarf (or a Twilly). Keyrings and other trinkets are not for elegant ladies.

Or, if you are keen on getting a classic, timeless designer piece, wait for a sale or check out pre-loved websites and exchange shops. But do your research and make sure they are authentic. Never buy fake merchandise!

If you have a large spending budget - it's entirely up to you - buy straight from the designer shop. But don't stretch your finances to get the latest designer bags because they are **not essential** in your transformation!

NOTES:
- When you start networking, you will be invited to various events, and you should have the following bags:

- ✓ Two tote bags (one in light, one in dark colour) - for everyday activities
- ✓ A crossbody (or two) - for casual activities
- ✓ A day clutch for formal daytime events
- ✓ An evening clutch for evening events
- ✓ A casual weekend bag for overnight stays
- ✓ A beach bag for holidays in the sun

- Your bags should be structured with clean lines and sleek designs
- At the beginning of your transformation, buy only the essential bags

~ 38 ~

CAPSULE WARDROBE

The pieces in each category listed below are things you can combine to create unlimited numbers of everyday outfits.

Shop smart, get high-quality items and resume to the list below. After you finish creating a complete capsule wardrobe with all the essentials on the list, you can purchase statement pieces **ONLY** if you find something you love!

Don't buy statement pieces before you have a complete capsule wardrobe! For example, buying your winter coat in a bold colour or with heavy patterns will limit what you can accessorise it with.

However, having a beige fitted winter coat, you can play around with all kinds of accessories, from delicate silk scarves tied around your neck to oversized wool shawls draped over your coat. You can also add belts to the coat or wear it with various hats in all colours because you will not find many colours that clash with beige.

So, that's why it's essential to create a capsule wardrobe! You have to be able to combine your pieces in numerous ways. And you cannot do that easily with bold statement pieces.

Also, after your capsule wardrobe is complete, only buy items if they look good on you and if you fall head over heels in love with them!

If you don't fall in love with them, you may not wear them often enough.

If something you bought doesn't look good on you, wearing it just because you bought it will be a mistake. You must learn to dress in a way that makes you look flawless. And throwing clothes on without consideration will rarely make you exquisite.

Impulsive buying is a habit that you must learn to get rid of!

But, before any statement pieces, here is a list of the items covered in the previous chapters to complete your capsule wardrobe:

Underwear
- t-shirt bras for comfortable everyday use (your skin colour, white and black)
- sports bras for physical exercise (in your skin colour, white and black)
- strapless bras and multi-way bras for Bardot, strapless or halterneck tops and dresses (in your skin colour, white and black)
- full cup stick-on bras for backless dresses (in your skin colour, white and black); never get silicone stick-on bras - they are not classy

- for large-chested women, balconette bras for support (in your skin colour, white and black)
- several pairs of nude and seamless knickers for light-coloured clothes
- matching knickers and bras in your desired colours for intimate playtime

Tops, blouses, and shirts

- one crisp white long-sleeve fitted shirt made from high-quality cotton
- one crisp blue long-sleeve fitted shirt made from high-quality cotton
- one white oversized linen shirt (to wear over camisoles and summer dresses)
- one off-white, ivory or cream-coloured silk blouse (for your body shape) to create sophisticated daytime outfits
- one navy, red or other dark colour silk blouse (for your body shape) to create sophisticated evening outfits
- few pastel-coloured tops and blouses to combine with your trousers and skirts
- light fabric camisoles in various colours
- fine cashmere or merino wool turtlenecks in white, black and nude (for pairing them up with other

separates to instantly elevate an
outfit in every season)
- cashmere and wool jumpers and
sweaters in dark and light colours for
the colder months

Skirts
After deciding the structure and length that
flatter your body shape, choose from the
following types, but **only the ones that suit
you**:
- pencil
- pleated
- straight
- A-line
- layered
- asymmetrical
- draped
- wrap

Dresses
- pencil dress (or sheath dress) in a
  dark colour (preferably black or navy
  blue) to create various outfits for
  informal events and activities, both
  day and evening
- pencil dress (or sheath dress) in a
  light colour (beige, cream, off-white,
  ivory, champagne) to create various
  outfits mainly for daytime wear
- knee-length cocktail dress
  (preferably in a darker colour and of

a flowy material) for dates and
informal evening events
- pastel-coloured summer dress (above
the knee, knee-length or midi) for
everyday use in the summer
- maxi beach dress (white or in a light
colour) for picnics or holidays in the
sun
- smart casual long-sleeve dress in a
thicker fabric to wear on colder days

Trousers and jeans
Choose from the following list **only** what
suits your body shape:
- tailored trousers
- classic pleated trousers
- narrow leg trousers
- wide leg trousers
- straight leg trousers
- cigarette trousers
- palazzo trousers
- high-waisted trousers
- bootcut jeans
- straight jeans
- slim jeans
- skinny jeans (only if your legs are
slender and your calves are thin)

Blazers and jackets
- a fitted black (or navy) blazer (single
or double-breasted, depending on
your body shape

- a tweed fitted blazer in a slightly lighter colour, such as dark olive or tawny
- a linen blazer in a light colour such as ivory, off-white or pastel to wear with the sleeves ruched or rolled up (while the first two blazers look best fitted, you should get the linen blazer one size up for a more relaxed yet elegant summer look)
- a quilted or wax jacket in a dark colour such as black, navy blue, brown, dark grey or dark green

Coats
- one long tailored coat in black
- one long tailored coat in beige, off-white, cream or another light colour
- one trench coat in a dark colour
- one trench coat in a light colour

Footwear
- several pairs of pumps with various size heels, from flat to high heels (in nude, brown, navy, black, grey and perhaps red)
- two pairs of sandals with mid-length or low heels (one nude and one white); because you may be walking more in summer
- one pair or two pairs of wedges and some pretty flip-flops (find flip-flops

ornated with something like
rhinestones or other stylish details;
but in good taste, nothing over the
top)
- one pair of simple, stylish sports
  shoes (in white or cream)
- one pair of knee-high boots with
  mid-height or lower heels (in a
  neutral colour)
- one pair of ankle boots with mid-
  height or lower heels (in a neutral
  colour)

Accessories

- a set of pearls (neckless and earrings
  or pendant and earrings)
- two delicate sets of gold pendants
  and studs (one in white gold and one
  in yellow gold, preferably; but if you
  can only afford one set, opt for white
  gold as it's classier)
- a subtle, precious stone pendant and
  earrings (or a set with a semiprecious
  stone, if diamonds or other precious
  stones are too much over your
  budget)
- elegant gloves in a few colours
- belts of various widths in black,
  caramel brown, nude and white
- scarves and hats in different colours

- sunglasses to suit the shape of your face
- tights in nude and black

Bags
• a black structured tote bag
• a light-coloured (such as cream or beige) structured tote bag
• a crossbody (if you can only get one, go for black, dark grey or other dark colours; when you are comfortable purchasing your second crossbody, you can choose a lighter neutral colour)
• a day clutch (if you can only get one, go for nude or off-white)
• an evening clutch (a dark colour would be a good choice, or if you wish, you can go for something sparkly - but keep it classy!)
• a casual weekend bag
• a beach bag (canvas or straw)

~ 39 ~

CHOOSING YOUR PERFUME

If you have a perfume you wear and everyone loves on you, that should be your signature scent.

Having a signature scent that people associate with you is very classy. However, some people prefer to have several perfumes.

It's OK if you want to have only one or to have more perfumes, but you must choose them correctly.

Plan to go for perfume testing early in the morning.

First, shower, and don't put any perfume or strong-smelling lotion on your skin before trying on a new fragrance, as this can alter the composition you're about to test.

Also, trying only one new perfume at a time would be best. If you have a particular one in mind, spray a little on the wrist and the back of your hand (if you wear long sleeves) or inside your elbow (if you wear short sleeves). Not many people choose to do the test on the back of the hand, but I think it's a good idea to do so because if you spray on the wrist and the sleeve rubs on it, the first notes evaporate and will interfere with the final fragrance. Also, spray some inside the elbow, only if, at the time of testing, you wear short sleeves to let it dry naturally, as anything rubbing against freshly applied perfume will get rid of the top notes.

Don't rub the perfume after spraying it on your skin, as it will destroy the small molecules of the more delicate top notes.

You have to allow it to dry naturally, and you should sniff your wrist and the back of your hand throughout the day to see how the fragrance develops.

If you tested it in the morning, you would know if you love or hate it by early evening. If you are not in love with the perfume, don't buy it!

The next day, or another day when it's convenient, go to the shop early in the morning, pick another perfume and start the same process until you find the one you love. Only wear perfumes **after** trying them! Find fragrances that you (and the people who smell them on you) love.

The Top Notes
The top notes (opening notes or headnotes) are the lightest ones.
The top notes are recognised immediately after the application and have a light molecular structure. They are the first to evaporate but are still a significant factor in

the final result of the fragrance. The top notes are the ones that "draw" you in when you try on a new perfume, which is why you sometimes discover that a scent that perhaps didn't entice you immediately became much more pleasant later in the day.

The most common fragrance top notes are ginger, lemon, orange zest, bergamot, grapefruit, berries, sage, and lavender.

The Middle Notes
The middle notes are considered the heart notes and start appearing once the top notes evaporate, influencing the final base notes. Standard middle notes: cinnamon, carnation, jasmine, nutmeg, coriander, cardamom, lemongrass, geranium, May rose, ylang-ylang, neroli, pine, rose, lily, orchid and lavender.

The Base Notes
The base notes (or the dry-down) are the final fragrance notes, and they are the ones that last the longest on the skin, providing a lasting impression. They appear once the top notes dissipate entirely and, together with the heart notes, create the full body of the fragrance.

Typical fragrances for base notes include cedarwood, sandalwood, vanilla, amber, oakmoss, musk, myrrh, patchouli, and Ylang Ylang.

Understanding what each note means is essential to finding the perfect fragrance for you. Choosing a perfume is not only about each note. It is about how the notes blend to form the fragrance's character. You must find ingredients that appeal to you and scents which suit your style.

Don't let people choose for you, because choosing a perfume is very personal.

The perfumes are mixtures of essential oils and aromas, which will vary from person to person when applied to the skin.

Then, each of us has an "emotional imprint" in our nerve cells, which may be why our brain associates certain smells with people and experiences from the past. So while your friend may associate a fragrance with a beautiful memory from her childhood, you may have a different experience when you try the same perfume for the first time.

And also, don't wear a specific perfume just because everyone else is wearing it. Not all trends suit everyone.

Keep your perfumes outside the bathroom and out of the sunlight in a cool, dry, dark place.

~ 40 ~

DRESS CODES

There are many dress codes used for various occasions. I will write about the ones you'll hear the most and give only the women's requirements for each dress code since it is very likely that, if a gentleman invites you to any of the events, he will know what to wear. But if you are new to this and want to see what your male companion will wear on each occasion, research and find out.

If you attend an event with a dress code not mentioned on the list below, google the specific dress code to see what you need to wear, or ask the host/organisers.

Understanding the basic dress codes is essential, as you don't want to turn up somewhere dressed inappropriately and feel like you don't belong.

WHITE TIE

White tie ("full evening dress", "tails", or "dress suit") is the most formal of dress codes, and it's worn in the evening at certain royal ceremonies, state or livery ceremonies, balls or banquets and Oscars. Also, specific formal evening weddings and charity balls may request a white tie dress code.

What women wear:

- full-length, formal evening dresses only (shorter dresses or trousers are unacceptable)
- long evening gloves are traditional, but they are not compulsory anymore, depending on the event
- hair is worn up
- small, elegant evening bags
- dazzling jewellery, even tiaras
- evening coat, cloak or a wrap (of suitable material)

There are different variations on the White Tie dress code (depending on the culture or the formality of the event), and it would be stated on the invitation.

If you wear gloves, you can keep them on when shaking hands or dancing, but remove them when you eat. Never eat anything with your gloves on! Instead, you remove them finger by finger and place them on your lap, underneath your napkin.

BLACK TIE

Black tie dress code, less formal than white tie, is the most frequently encountered formal evening wear, worn for dinners (both public and private), parties and balls.

What women wear:
- long evening dress (silk, crepe, chiffon, velvet, lace, satin)
- blouse and a long skirt or floaty evening trousers are now accepted, but I would still advise wearing a long evening dress
- fine or costume jewellery, but not tiaras
- elegant evening bag
- evening coat, cloak, or shawl

MORNING DRESS

Morning dress is also known as "formal day dress" and is traditional at weddings, formal memorial services, some official functions and formal daytime events.

What women wear:
- smart day dress or skirt with jacket, bolero or shawl
- the dress/skirt should not be too short/revealing
- opt for wedges, or a mid/low heel, instead of high heels
- tights or stockings
- pearls or other daytime jewellery
- hats are traditional

LOUNGE SUIT

Lounge suits are worn for most business events (daytime and evening) and social events such as lunches, dinners, receptions, christenings, weddings and funerals.

What women wear:

a) For events happening during the day:

- Knee-length day dress, skirt and jacket or trouser suit

b) For events happening in the evening:

- smart or cocktail dress (with sleeves or worn with a jacket)

COCKTAIL

The cocktail dress code is for semi-formal evening functions and parties

What women wear:

- dress (knee length or just above the knee) or an evening trouser suit
- high heels
- playful and sophisticated accessories
- chic evening bag

SMART CASUAL

This dress code doesn't have many rules, so think of it as polished, yet relaxed. It's a step up from casual attire.

What women wear:

- smart day dress and jacket, or trousers/skirt with a cardigan
- skirt and blouse/shirt

- simple jeans and smart blazer can also pull a smart casual look
- flat shoes or heels, both are suitable
- smart accessories
- sportswear is NOT adequate!

PARTIES / FESTIVE ATTIRE

Sometimes events requiring this dress code may be fancy or have a theme. Usually, the theme is stated on the invitation, and you should respect the requests of your host. If you feel uncomfortable wearing an entire outfit in the chosen theme, you can at least wear something smart and pick an accessory or a piece of jewellery to show that you made an effort.

A few other dress codes are more relaxed than smart casual, but I will not write about them, because we should only wear sportswear if we are doing any sportive events or training. And we should never find ourselves being "TOO CASUAL" in public.

If most of your everyday outfits are smart casual, then you have mastered the art of elegance.

41

POSTURE AND DEPORTMENT

Posture is the way one holds one's body when sitting or standing.
Deportment refers to how one carries and conducts oneself, the way one walks, to one's demeanour and mannerisms.

Most people are unaware of their posture; therefore, they don't know if it's good or bad. So before you start improving yours, film yourself standing and sitting relaxed to understand where you are in terms of posture and what needs adjusting.

Leave your recording camera on for a few hours while you do things around the house so that you can see yourself in different sitting and standing positions.

By becoming aware of your current sitting and standing posture, you will know what to address and correct.

Then, you will learn to keep your back straight all the time and find that slouching is uncomfortable. You won't be able to sit or walk with a slouch again.

Film yourself from separate angles and walk as you would normally do, in different shoes, to see your current posture.

Then, exercise walking with what you think is a good posture.

When you feel that you can walk with grace, re-record yourself.

See the difference between the recordings and make the necessary changes to master your posture.

Walk with grace, even if you are at home in your slippers.

Only when you are elegant with no one seeing you can genuinely say you have mastered the art of being a lady.

How to walk elegantly:

1) Stand tall and carry yourself with confidence.
Imagine a string running through your spine to the top of your head, forcing you to keep your body straight.

2) Pull your shoulders back, hold your head high and your chin parallel to the ground, and tuck your tummy in.
It should not feel uncomfortable if you are slim and fit.
If you are not slim and fit, go back to the chapter covering the required sizes for this project: sizes 8, 10, and 12 (for average and tall heights) or size 6 (if you are petite). If you are slim, tucking your tummy in shouldn't feel uncomfortable. However, if your stomach is too large to be tucked in, you must get into shape.

3) Keep your arms relaxed by your side, and don't fidget with your hands and fingers. Don't try to find something elaborate to do with your arms while you're walking, as it is little you can do with them. Instead, keep them relaxed by your side and don't cross them over your chest, don't walk with them in your back pockets or do anything unusual. Just be relaxed and let your arms fall naturally by your sides.

4) Take smooth, medium-length strides. Not too short, as that would make you look insecure and nervous. And not too long, as it would make you look clumsy.
You can try walking by putting a foot directly in front of the other to give your hips that seductive little swing, but don't

cross your legs in an exaggerated way when you walk, as you can either seem like you're trying too hard, or your walk may look too sexual.

If putting a foot directly in front of the other is too complicated, keep your toes pointing forward and walk, forming two imaginary parallel lines. Avoid the "duck feet walk" that makes your feet point outward.

You don't need the aggressive powerwalk to give you confidence. Instead, you can project confidence by being feminine and relaxed and having a slow and steady walk. Walk confidently, and don't look at your feet.

5) Look ahead. Don't frown; keep your forehead relaxed and have a subtle smile at all times (unless you attend a sad event, where smiling would be inappropriate). Even if your face is stern, you should never frown.

Learn to walk in high heels. Of course, no one says that you should walk in the highest heels, but there are outfits which are significantly complemented by a pair of high heels, and it would be a shame to miss out on an opportunity to look truly elegant.

When sitting down:

Keep your knees together when you sit down and lock them so you don't show up your skirt, and never allow your legs to relax and part, making you look masculine. Check the correct way to get in and out of the car without flashing your underwear. Practise when you are alone, as you may have to do this a few times before you get the hang of it and become mindful of the process.

After learning to be elegant, it becomes your second nature, and you will always be elegant, not only in the presence of others.

Do fewer things and do them with elegance. Rushing to do many things at once is rarely efficient and never elegant!

Give yourself enough time to do tasks and get to your destinations without rushing.

If you need to attend an event, you should visit the restroom on arrival at the venue to ensure that you look composed and that your makeup and hair look tidy. It is unpleasant to burst into a room looking flustered and dishevelled while everyone else is poised and relaxed. You want to stand out and look good.

You enter the room, confident and relaxed and with a smile on your face. Take a moment to glance and familiarise yourself with the room, locate the person you are meant to meet and go straight to them.
If they are conversing with someone else, do not interrupt. Instead, position yourself at an angle to be seen by your host, make eye contact, smile and let them come to you.
Then, get a drink so you don't stand around awkwardly, and the host will come to you to introduce you to people or show you where you have to sit.

If you are meeting someone for a date and the proposed location is a restaurant, you don't enter the restaurant floor and try to locate your date yourself.
The last thing you want to do is embarrass yourself and your date by looking like a lost sheep between tables. Mention the name of the booking at the reception and wait to be taken to the table.

These seemingly minor details done incorrectly will make you feel like you don't belong. So, the more attention you pay to these details, the faster you learn to be part of the elite. Watch and learn from others and implement the rules, as people will judge you by how you present yourself.

42

TABLE MANNERS

It doesn't matter how formal or casual the dinner is; there are some things you never do!

- DON'T talk with food in your mouth!
- DON'T put your elbows on the table!
- DON'T slouch!
- DON'T slurp!
- DON'T drink while you still have food in your mouth!
- DON'T gesture with your cutlery while talking!
- DON'T scrape the cutlery against your plate or your teeth!
- DON'T lift your elbows and eat with them raised in the air! Instead, your wrists should be kept low and your elbows tucked in, close to your body. This way, you have more control over problematic foods (spaghetti, rice, lobster, oysters etc.) and remain elegant while eating them.

If you are dining in a restaurant, as soon as you sit down, unfold your napkin, fold it again in half and place it on your lap. There are some restaurants where the waiter opens the napkin and places it on your lap, in which case, you sit back gently while they do that, and then, you look at them and thank them.

However, if you are invited for dinner at someone's house, you wait for the host to indicate where to sit, and then you wait for them to start unfolding their napkin before you begin doing so.

If you need to leave the table during dinner, you excuse yourself and fold your napkin so that you don't leave your lipstick or food stains on show, as it would be an unpleasant sight for the rest of the guests at the table. You leave your napkin on your chair. When you finish the meal, the napkin is folded loosely and placed on the left side of the plate.

You have your butter plate on your left and your glass on your right. If you ever need to remember the glass and bread plate placement, put your hands on the table and bring your index fingers to touch your thumbs while the other fingers remain pointing straight up.
You will notice that:
- the left hand formed the letter "b" from "bread"

- the right hand formed the letter "d" from "drink"

This way, whenever you sit at a large table with many guests and need clarification about your butter plate and water glass, you can do this exercise discreetly to remind yourself that the bread plate is on your left and the drink is on your right.

The forks are positioned on the left-hand side, and knives and spoons are on the right-hand side of your plate.

You start using your cutlery from the outside, working your way in.

Never place used cutlery back on the table. Instead, always rest them on your plate while you pause to say something during the course or after your meal. While resting, place the cutlery at 3:40, with the bridge of the fork (tines down) over the knife's blade.

When finished, the cutlery is placed at:
- 6:30, with the blade of the knife inward and the tines of the fork facing **up** (British etiquette)
- 4:20, with the blade of the knife inward and the tines of the fork facing **up** (American etiquette)

- 3:15, with the blade of the knife inward and the tines of the fork facing **down** (European etiquette)

It's not a major faux pas if you use either of the finishing positions for the cutlery, but if you can't remember how they do it in other parts of the world, stick with the way Brits do it: placement at 6:30.

Spoon
If you are having soup, you use your right hand to scoop away from you and eat the soup from the side of the spoon closest to you. Don't hit the plate with the spoon or slurp the soup.
When resting, the spoon is placed on the right, on the charger plate (or the base plate, service plate or underplate).
After finishing, the spoon is placed at 6:30 (or 4:20 or 3:15).

Knife and fork
For the main course, the knife and fork should NOT be used as if they were pens.
Instead, place your index fingers down the knife and the fork in a flat position, not forming an arch.
The finger on the fork should stop just before the bridge of the fork.
The finger on the knife should stop just before the blade of the knife.

The handles should be inside your palms, not held like pens.

If you pause during the course, you place the cutlery at 3:40, the knife's blade facing inward and the bridge of the fork resting over the blade of the knife, tines facing down.

When finished, you place the cutlery side by side at 6:30, knife with the blade facing inward and the fork at the left of the knife, tines facing up. (In America: 3:40, with the blade of the knife inward and the tines of the fork up, in Europe: 3:15, with the blade of the knife inward and the tines of the fork down.)

Cutlery for the Sweet Course
You should use a spoon and a fork while eating the sweet course. As before, when pausing, your fork and spoon should rest on the plate at 3:40, and when you finish, you place the cutlery at 6:30. Or, if you are in other parts of the world, you can use their custom.

Note: British upper class don't really use the word "dessert". They prefer to use "pudding", which can be sweet or savoury.

If you have to bring food from a platter, use the cutlery on the platter to transfer to your plate and then use your cutlery to cut and eat the food. Never use your cutlery to take food from a serving platter.

When you are invited to a dinner party, don't be a demanding guest, as that would reflect poorly on you, and you may not be invited next time.
For example, asking for coffee when you arrive is inconsiderate. Instead, wait until the coffee is served at the end of the meal. The host is probably busy getting started on serving the aperitifs, and any extra demands would not be welcome.

Also, if you go to someone for dinner, always bring something. However, if you get flowers, choose a bunch that comes with water, so the host doesn't have to go through the inconvenience of finding a vase when other things are more important.

There are many rules to learn regarding etiquette and good manners, and you should never think you know enough. When you feel that you have mastered the etiquette of your culture, always study the etiquette of other cultures. People will be grateful and very impressed to see that you know about their traditions and customs.

But before you educate yourself about other cultures, make sure you understand the basic etiquette rules in the country where you live.

Remember that being rich doesn't necessarily guarantee impeccable manners. Some rich people may not have impeccable manners. But that doesn't mean you can get away with not having them. You must elevate yourself to such a level that you would be confident to dine with Royalty. Even if it's a casual meal with friends or if you dine with people who don't master table manners, you must respect the DON'Ts at the beginning of the chapter.

And because you are an elegant woman, you must remember that you should never make someone feel bad for their table manners. So if someone specifically asks you to teach them, you can do so, but never take it upon yourself to point out what they do wrong.

Remember, having good manners is about how you make others feel in your presence.

An excellent etiquette expert is William Hanson. I recommend you follow his advice to educate yourself on further etiquette and civility.

43

LEARN TO BE ELEGANT

As you build your new wardrobe, find where sample sales are held or wait for seasonal sales in good stores. When buying things, don't opt for trends; instead, buy timeless pieces. You don't need to change your wardrobe every season! In fact, no one should change their wardrobe every season, as we should all be more mindful of the environment and buy fewer things of higher quality!

Use the January sale (or other significant sales) to top up your wardrobe with things you need, but don't purchase clothes randomly just because they are reduced. Instead, get only things which, after trying on and fitting perfectly, you are confident you will wear them.

As you learned in the "Capsule Wardrobe" chapter, you must learn to dress flawlessly, even in the simplest clothes. By throwing ill-fitting clothes on, you will downgrade your look.

Try and buy high-end items whenever you can (either when a sale is on or from designer outlets, exchange shops or other online platforms) because the quality of the materials is generally higher, and the tailoring is much better.

You can find excellent pieces from past collections if you focus on timeless cuts rather than trends. Buy less but buy quality!

Another option is finding a good seamstress or sewist. There are people with incredible talent for creating beautiful clothes at a fraction of what you would pay in a designer store. That way, you can buy high-quality materials and have custom-made garments to fit you perfectly. A seamstress or sewist is necessary for your contact list, even for adjusting or repairing clothes when needed.

Remember that clothes don't have to be branded to have high quality and elegance. They need to fit you well and make you look elegant and comfortable. Educate yourself about genuine elegance and create an immaculate image to suit you.

Avoid prominent logos. Wearing flashy brands makes you look vulgar, and people will not think you are wealthy just because your logos are on show. Instead, they will feel that you lack good taste and sophistication. People who can afford to wear brands don't need to show it!

Elegance is NOT old-fashioned.

Elegance means dressing in a way that empowers and dignifies you while maintaining your personality and style. And when you learn how to do that successfully, you will never want to return to looking frumpy or too provocative.

Find elegant women of your age and get inspired by what they wear, and of course, remember to add your personal touch.

Use the names given as examples in the ROLE MODELS section. Observe their deportment and how they talk and take inspiration from them regarding outfits but create your unique style.

Your new capsule wardrobe should be much smaller if you have disposed of everything worn, ripped, or discoloured, as taught in the previous chapters. Moreover, it should contain high-quality materials and separates in various colours, which you can combine effortlessly to create numerous classy looks.

The essence of elegance really is simplicity.

For example, wearing a pair of trousers in a pastel colour and a top of the same shade, paired with beautiful shoes, will make you look elegant. Your skin, hair and nails are immaculate; all you need is a touch of lipstick, some tasteful jewellery, a sleek bag and a confident but gentle attitude.

Never wear leggings, tracksuits, or any sports gear if you are not exercising or going to exercise. The same goes for trainers. Sportswear should be worn only for sport, as no rich man wearing a suit or proper attire will approach you if you walk around in your sportswear. You will only attract people who are comfortable going out in tracksuits and trainers. And you may find that classy rich people do not fall into this category. You will attract some men if you look fit, but they may differ from the type of men you want.

Choose your clothes mindfully. If you start shopping for high-quality clothes, the prices will be higher, and you will learn to refrain from impulsive buying.

You will choose fewer clothes, spend more time trying them before deciding, and make better choices. As a result, your wardrobe will be smaller but of higher quality.

And you can combine different pieces, style them, and accessorise them properly. And once you get the hang of it, you will have much fun doing it. You don't need a personal stylist for your everyday wear. Every woman should learn to understand what suits her, so she can easily avoid any significant faux pas.

The wardrobe subject is incredibly vast, but assuming that the budget is limited for most of you at the beginning of your transformation, you will have to start prioritising accordingly.

Create folders on your phone with the titles "Spring", "Summer", "Autumn", "Winter", "Smart Casual", "Cocktail", "Evening", etc.

Take each name suggested in the ROLE MODELS section and Google images of their outfits, pick your favourites, and save them in the relevant folder. And every time you see an elegant outfit, take a picture, and keep it in your folders to inspire you the next time you shop for clothes.

That way, when you see a beautiful top, you will know what to combine it with to look good. So, **build your wardrobe on your phone first and in your cupboard after.**

If you dress with style when going out but look unkempt in the house (with or without your partner), you can't call yourself an elegant woman. You are just a woman who, OCCASIONALLY, dresses elegantly.

So, upgrade your house clothes as well, or at least get rid of any items which have holes and are discoloured or stained. Keep the clothes you wear at home simple and in good taste.

And finally, remember your deportment, speech and manners. Elegance is not just about wearing beautiful clothes for people to admire. Elegance is also about how you conduct yourself and about how you respect yourself and others, even when no one is looking.

Keep a healthy size, prioritise hygiene, keep your makeup simple and elevate your deportment, speech, and etiquette!

44

ROLE MODELS

The most common mistake many women make is choosing the wrong people as role models.

If you want more chances to meet high-value men, you must become a woman liked by **most high-value men**. You don't want to be a woman liked only by **a few men**.

Here is why:

FIRST SCENARIO:

Imagine you are in a room with 100 rich single men of various ages, sizes, and levels of attractiveness.

You come dressed very provocatively, and you flirt with everyone because you believe that just because Marilyn Monroe was admired by many, it must be the right way of attracting men. So, yes, you will attract many looks, but you will not necessarily attract many men!

The men in the room will fall into three categories:

1) men who may see this behaviour as inappropriate and will not come to speak to you (**men - NOT interested**)

2) men who will admire you from afar, but because they are embarrassed by this public display of provocativeness, they will not approach you (**men - NOT interested**)

3) men who will admire you and not be embarrassed to come and speak to you (**men - interested**)

So, even though many men may admire you, most will stay away.

This is the first selection, and you have no control over it as the men in the room make the selection, not you. As a result, you lost the interest of the men in the first two categories.

The men in the 3rd category (who will approach you) are separated into two subcategories:

3a) men interested only in a bit of fun (since you gave the impression that you are a "fun" woman) (**you - NOT interested**)

3b) men who may be interested in getting to know you better (**you - MAYBE interested**)

The second selection is made by you. But, by now, you only have a small subcategory.

So, after losing two main categories, 1 and 2 (men who were put off by your behaviour and those who were embarrassed to be seen approaching you), and after eliminating 3a (who were looking just for fun), you are left with a small subcategory: 3b. Therefore, you have very few choices.

So, to recap:
You had 100 people in the room.
Some didn't like your provocative demeanour. **(they eliminated you)**
Some didn't mind your demeanour but were embarrassed to be seen approaching you. **(they eliminated you)**
Some responded to your flirts and approached you. **(they chose you)**
Some (from the ones who approached you) were interested only in sex. **(you eliminated them)**
Some (from the ones who approached you) were interested in getting to know you. **(your left choices)**

Out of 100 men to start with, you are probably down to one or two genuinely interested in you.
What do you think about those one or two men?
Do you find them attractive and like their character?

Do you see them as suitable for potential partners?
If yes, then you have one or two phone numbers.
But if you don't find them appropriate, you may have to leave the room of 100 people without a single phone number.

SECOND SCENARIO:

Imagine that you are in a room with 100 rich single men of various ages, sizes, and levels of attractiveness.

You arrive tastefully dressed, stand tall and walk confidently; your hair is fabulous, and your make-up is subtle and accentuates your best features. You smile, and your face is luminous. You are the epitome of elegance. You attract many looks for all the right reasons.

All the men will likely be intrigued by you and want to get to know you.
One or two of the 100 men may be unchivalrous (**you eliminate them**).
The rest are gentlemen waiting for your interest. (**your left choices**)

In this scenario, you are making the selection from plenty of choices!

Wouldn't you want to be able to choose out of 98 men (second scenario) rather than 2 men (first scenario)? It's simple maths!

***

Rich men are super-achievers and seek very high standards from the woman they date. And the exaggerated display of sexiness is not considered a high standard. If outrageous behaviour is what they see first, they are not interested in knowing the rest. So, if you want them to be interested in you, don't drive them away! Instead, be elegant and show them that you are a suitable partner.

The above statement shouldn't outrage anyone because, as long as no one is hurt and the act is not illegal or immoral, a man or a woman should be allowed to like whom they like. So, if you read here that rich men prefer classy women, but you want to be provocative (or maybe tomboyish), don't let this upset you. Be as you wish! There are plenty of other available men in the world!

However, if you want to appeal to classy men and need the inspiration to elevate yourself, choose your role models wisely! For example, you may admire someone's courage for something they do, but you wouldn't necessarily copy their behaviour. Most people you know have some good traits you admire, but not everyone is your role model.

The role models you want to emulate should be the ones you admire entirely: from how they look to how they behave towards others to how they hold their values and principles.

Choose your role models wisely!

An example of a wrong role model is the protagonist of "Breakfast at Tiffany's" - a fabulous movie that deserves its place among the classics. Still, the character Holly Golightly is not exactly the epitome of elegance.
Holly is stylishly dressed but does not fall under the category of women with class and impeccable manners.
Therefore, the character of Holly Golightly from "Breakfast at Tiffany's" dresses well, but her bad principles don't classify her as an elegant woman and a role model.

And if you have any doubts, watch the film again and pay attention to everything she does and how she conducts herself. Holly is a party girl with her life in disarray.

This book teaches you precisely the opposite: **to be a dignified woman with your life in order.** "Breakfast at Tiffany's" is a sweet romantic film, and it's a pleasure to watch, but don't look for tips on the protagonist's behaviour! She is NOT a good role model!

However, the actress who played Holly Golightly, the fabulous Audrey Hepburn, was exquisite in every way. So, use her as an example for your studies.

In 1961, when Audrey Hepburn was attending a charity event in London, she was asked by an interviewer if Holly (the role she played in "Breakfast at Tiffany's") was anything like her. The actress smiled and said: "I'm not quite that way."

So, enjoy the film, but don't use it as inspiration. Instead, learn from the actress's life off-screen because Audrey Hepburn was a fantastic role model, a fashion icon, and a humanitarian.

Watch her interviews and study her mannerism, posture, the gentle way she spoke, her impeccable image and the way she preserved her timeless beauty throughout her life.

And if you haven't watched "My Fair Lady", watch it immediately or watch it again if you watched it in the past. "My Fair Lady" is a good study of the most extraordinary transformation of an unpolished, uneducated flower girl into a refined lady.

- **Audrey Hepburn** is an excellent example of inspiration, so find everything you can about her work and style because she will always be a worthy role model.

- **Amal Clooney** is an example of elegance, class, refinement, intelligence, and everything you can wish to achieve as a woman. Yes, she married George Clooney, which can be listed as an outstanding achievement, but George Clooney is fortunate to be married to such an incredible woman.

Amal was one of the most successful lawyers of her generation before she met her husband. She did not need the fame that came with marrying George, but she did not let that fame get in the way of her career. Instead, she used it to raise awareness of global human rights causes.

Amal is the embodiment of elegance and refinement.

I recommend you search for images of her outfits, but you should also watch some of the YouTube videos where she appears, so you can learn from her gestures, make-up, the way she talks, the way she smiles, her femininity and her humbleness. Learn everything from Amal Clooney, who epitomises sophistication, elegance, and class.

- **Queen Rania of Jordan** is an excellent humanitarian known for her advocacy work on health, education, and youth. She said in an interview that "with every passing year, things I wish for get smaller and simpler."

Watch everything that Queen Rania does: from the way she dresses, wears her make-up and hair, to the way she walks, talks, sits, smiles, and interacts with people.

- **Kate Middleton**, after she got married and became the Duchess of Cambridge.

Like any royal, she was taught the highest standards of manners and conduct, so observing how she dresses, walks, talks, and does her make-up and hair would help anyone who wants to elevate themselves. From whom better to learn, if not from the royals?! Watch Kate's way of engaging with people. She is present and warm and makes people feel important. Learning to master the quality of making people feel important is incredible.

Watch Kate Middleton (after she became The Duchess of Cambridge) for inspiration on how to dress, do your make-up and your hair, walk, and talk.

Other royals to use as inspiration for their sense of style:
- **Princess Madeleine of Sweden**
- **Princess Mary of Denmark**
- **Queen Mathilde of Belgium**
- **Queen Letizia of Spain**

Other women in the public eye that you can Google for fashion style inspiration:
- **Brigitte Macron** was a figure skater before she was a teacher, and she certainly knows how to preserve her figure admirably.

Google images of Brigitte Macron's outfits, and if you are a younger woman, don't think she is too old, and her style may not suit you. The woman can pull off jeans and stilettos with the same success as she pulls off a sharp blazer suit! I don't know much about her character, but no one can deny her incredible fashion sense.

Use as inspiration Brigitte Macron's outfits.

- **Meghan Markle** (for her sense of style when she was part of the royal family)

TV characters that you can take some inspiration from:
- **Charlotte York** (the character from "Sex And The City")

Charlotte is prim and proper, well-spoken, and dresses well. Her character is underrated in the series because Carrie is considered a fashionista. Still, Charlotte is the one who ticks most of the boxes in the elegance department, and her style is timeless. Her blunders are very few.

- **Jessica Pearson**, the character from the TV series "Suits".

I know little about the actress who played the role or her style outside the show, so I am not recommending the actress (Gina Torres). Instead, I am recommending the character (Jessica Pearson). You will find stylish outfits if you watch the show, or Google images of Jessica Pearson's outfits. Use them as examples.

However, I am only talking about how Jessica Pearson dressed, not how she behaved at work.

Why?

Because Jessica was very tough, and she could afford to be like that, as she was very accomplished professionally and financially and didn't need a man to help her achieve her dreams.

If you were to behave like Jessica Pearson's character, you might be perceived as someone who doesn't want to be approached. And you certainly want to seem approachable, as your goal is to expand your network.

So, if you like Jessica Pearson's toughness, you can display it when you are as successful as she is. At the beginning of your transformation, be soft and gentle (and hopefully, you'll remain like that always, even when you are at the peak of your success).

Observe and take inspiration from how she dresses, her make-up and hair, and how she sits and walks. But don't copy her character.

***

Please note that not all the above names are suggested for role models. Some names are given to use as inspiration only for their sense of style.

Remember to differentiate between admiring certain traits in some people and looking up to people worthy of role models.

***

Finding celebrities who are constantly elegant is challenging. Stars are sometimes paid to follow trends, are involved in scandals, or play roles that may make them too sexual. Not all celebrities are as well-spoken as Audrey Hepburn was in her interviews, so they are not always a good source of inspiration if you want to learn the art of elocution and communication.

Also, they cannot be considered role models if scandal and controversy are attached to their names.

As a result, Marlyn Monroe is not on the list because, although an icon, Marlyn was too sexual. You don't want to be a woman who is too sexual.

You want to be memorised for your polished manners, gentleness, and dignified nature. The ultimate beauty is a combination of these three. An elegant woman exudes sex appeal when she doesn't try to be sexy; and when she is feminine but classy.

Marlyn Monroe may have played some elegant roles, but in real life, the actress didn't possess all the traits of class and elegance. So, enjoy her movies, and appreciate her beauty and charisma, but don't look for inspiration of refinement in Marlyn Monroe's life.

Seek inspiration from members of different royal families because it's easier to find royals whose elegance is constant. As a royal, one must abide by specific rules, and one cannot follow trends or show too much flesh. They take speech lessons, and most of their interviews are a good source of inspiration regarding the correct way to speak and communicate. Their involvement in various good causes makes them good ambassadors of compassion, a trait any elegant woman should possess.

Also, I didn't give any examples of role models in their 20s because it's harder to find women (in the public eye) between 18 and 30 with a constant image of elegance and class. Usually, very young women are much more casual. They are more likely to follow trends rather than opt for classic, timeless looks, which is why it takes more work to find a very young celebrity to include in this list. Of course, there are many elegant young women, but they may not necessarily be in the public eye.

So, if you are 20-something years old and want to begin your transformation, use the same role models mentioned above and pick outfits that look youthful and resonate with your personality. Young women can also be classy, elegant, and chic without looking old-fashioned.

And if you are very young, it is OK to be more daring, if you keep it in good taste. But if you are older, cover up more.

Elevating yourself into an elegant woman doesn't mean you must become old-fashioned. On the contrary, it means you become the most refined version of yourself. Whether a very young or mature woman, you can take inspiration from the role models in this section and add your personal touch for authenticity.

NOTES

Choose the following people as inspiration and learn from everything they do (from their fashion sense, hair, make-up, and posture to the way they speak, and they interact with others)
- The Duchess of Cambridge
- Queen Rania of Jordan
- Amal Clooney
- Audrey Hepburn
- Grace Kelly
- Princess Madeleine of Sweden
- Princess Mary of Denmark

- Queen Mathilde of Belgium
- Queen Letitia of Spain

And choose CERTAIN things as inspiration from the following people/characters:
- Meghan Markle, for her fashion sense, during her period with the Royals
- Brigitte Macron, for her fashion sense, only
- Charlotte York, for most of her style and conduct
- Jessica Pearson (the character from "Suits"), for her fashion sense, her hair, make-up, and her posture (not for her bossy attitude)

~ 45 ~

MENTORS

You need mentors in this project, and you need mentors in life in general.

The difference between role models and mentors is that your role models can help you with **setting up** goals and aspirations, while mentors are the ones who can help you **achieve** your goals and aspirations.

Role models can be either people you know, or people you've never met in your life who can help you indirectly while observing them. Mentors are people who know everything about you and can help you directly.

A mentor can be someone more experienced than you and willing to help. They listen to you and advise. And you must learn to treasure their time, knowledge, and feedback.

A mentor can be there to tell you what you do well and what needs to be changed so you can progress. They will listen to and guide you. But in return, you must show that you are making progress. If you don't progress, your mentor will not be there for you forever.

Just as important, it doesn't matter how close you become; you will not overwhelm your mentors with requests and will respect their time and privacy. After all, you can only become a classy lady if you apply the rules of good manners to friends and people close to you first.

Where do you find mentors?

After befriending a series of people met in various circumstances and with whom you formed a connection, look at the ones you are more drawn to because they genuinely want to see you grow. They are the ones giving you directions and encouraging you. Find the right time to ask them if they wouldn't mind guiding you in your journey.

Be honest about your desire to elevate yourself. You want to learn to be a refined woman who looks, talks, walks, and behaves as if she belongs among high-standard people.

Tell them you are willing to listen, learn and work hard to build a comfortable future for yourself, but you need guidance. Ask if they can help.

If your message is clear, truthful, and gentle (because you don't want to say something that makes you look desperate), they may be happy to help. A mentor is someone whose wisdom and experience can be groundbreaking in this process.

And don't worry if you don't always agree with your mentor, or sometimes you may want to make certain decisions independently. When you feel strongly, do what feels right for you at that moment, even if you make mistakes. From time to time, you must make mistakes to learn. But it's essential to acknowledge your wrongdoings and try to rectify them in future.

Be bold and ask questions if you don't know or need help understanding something. Asking questions is a sign of intelligence; no one will see it as a weakness. On the contrary, any intelligent person will admit they don't have all the answers. And what an outstanding achievement is when you become a better version of yourself with each passing day and with more acquired knowledge!

You can have many mentors, but choose them wisely, don't take them for granted and be grateful for having these special people in your life!

~ 46 ~

YOUR HOME

After decluttering your wardrobe, you must start decluttering your whole living space. Your transformation is incomplete if you upgrade your looks, behaviour, and general knowledge, but your home (which should be your haven) is cluttered and untidied. The transformation must include not only what people see; your inner self and your home should also go through a positive change.

As your network expands, you will start vising beautiful locations, and if, when you return home, things are piled up and scattered all over the place, you will become overwhelmed and dissatisfied with your life.

Everything around you will have to become Zen. And if you can "Zenify" as many things in your life as possible, you can deal much easier with something out of your control. So, to find inner peace, your home must be orderly, elegant, and spotless.

If you live alone, declutter all your house. If you live with people, completely declutter your bedroom and as much as you can from the common parts.

Your body needs good quality sleep to regenerate itself, and you must ensure you make that possible.

After reading Mathew Walker's book "Why We Sleep", Bill Gates wrote on his blog: "Walker, the director of UC Berkeley's

Center for Human Sleep Science, explains how neglecting sleep undercuts your creativity, problem-solving, decision-making, learning, memory, heart health, brain health, mental health, emotional well-being, immune system, and even your life span".

It is imperative that your diet, drinking and partying habits, state of mind and environment don't get in the way of getting a good night's sleep. Enough quality sleep will improve your mental and physical health and, ultimately, your life.

After organising things piled up in your bedroom and removing the unnecessary knick-knacks, remove the patterned and coloured bedlinen and replace them with white bed linen. Go for a higher thread count if you can, but if you cannot splash on something too expensive, at least make sure your bed linen is 100% cotton and it's white.

You are a grownup woman looking to elevate your lifestyle, and an elegant woman cannot spend 1/3 of her time sleeping on a bed which doesn't look and feel fabulous. Sleep is essential, so it should be peaceful and undisturbed.

If you cannot immediately go for bed linen of higher quality, you can find white bedsheets in budget stores (sometimes, even sets with higher thread count) but make sure they are 100% cotton. The higher thread count costs a little more than the ones with a lower thread count, but they cost much less than if you were to buy them from upmarket stores. So, check budget stores for white bed linen and get rid of any coloured and patterned sheets immediately!

And at the next big sale (especially in January), buy good quality white bed linen and white towels from a more upmarket department store.

Wrapping yourself in soft white towels after a shower and sleeping on quality sheets is luxurious. And it's a great way to start and end your day.

And if you find that it's too expensive to purchase a couple of silk pillowcases, find a fabric shop near you (or online) and buy enough silk material for two pillowcases and make them yourself at home, or ask a seamstress (sewist) to do them for you.

Sleeping on silk has anti-ageing benefits, reduces hair frizz, and feels luxurious. Remember to wash silk at a low temperature, while the rest of your cotton linen should be washed at 60C or above to eliminate dust mites. Wash your bed linen at least once a week and iron it before use. It is incredibly satisfying to sleep on crisp, clean sheets.

Choose a soothing, relaxing paint colour for your bedroom walls to calm a busy mind.

Don't place mirrors in a way that they face the bed (or cover them at night).

Keep things tidy and organised, and close drawers and wardrobe doors when not in use.

Don't keep a TV in your bedroom and limit the use of electronic devices just before going to bed.

Use low-light bulbs and if you can, invest in Himalayan salt lamps for your bedside tables. When heated, the salt crystal lamps emit negative ions that fight against electromagnetic radiation, and the purified air helps you achieve a good night's sleep. In addition, the beautiful glow acts as a mood elevator and a stress reliever.

Switch off your notifications or your Wi-Fi. Get your friends used to the hours you take calls, so they don't make a habit of calling you late at night. And, even if sometimes you may have an event which will keep you up late, maintain an overall good sleep routine.

The towels (like your bed linen and bathrobe) should be white, so you can feel fabulous after taking showers and baths. Keep your bathroom spotless, organise your creams and cosmetics in containers, and put them away in cabinets and cupboards.

If they are not flowers, lamps, pictures or art, all items in your house should have a home (stored away in cupboards and drawers), and your place should be neat.

In the kitchen, keep your crockery matching and remove plastic, chipped, discoloured or broken items. Regarding glasses, you can find beautiful and inexpensive crystal glasses through Amazon. When you break them, looking at past orders and getting the same ones will save you the hassle of having mismatched glasses. You can do the same with crockery.

Research how to declutter your house, keep things simple, and reduce the decision-making process. Then, consider applying some Feng Shui tips for creating a harmonious living space. Decluttering is easier than you think, and the satisfaction you get afterwards is worthwhile.

You must understand how crucial elevating your living space is in your transformation. So don't try to skip it!

Your home must bring you so much joy that you will be delighted to return even from the most luxurious holiday.

Write down the things you do at home:
- waking up
- showering
- getting dressed
- pampering yourself
- eating
- sleeping

And now, take them one by one and change things in your environment to ensure you experience optimal joy and satisfaction when doing them.
- You will wake up to a tidy bedroom and start your day in a great mood.
- You will love the incredible sensation of a clean, soft towel on your skin.
- You will not be overwhelmed by your skincare routine when you

remove unwanted makeup and creams and keep the essentials to maintain your skin healthy and protected.

- You will enjoy getting dressed when you have different folders in your phone with outfits for each occasion, and your clothes are correctly stored and easy to find.
- You will look forward to having relaxing baths in a decluttered bathroom.
- You will enjoy your meals more when eaten from simple but beautiful crockery.
- You will fall asleep with a positive mindset in your tranquil bedroom without all the distractions (the phone, TV, and random knick-knacks), and you will get restful sleep, preparing you for another happy and prosperous day.

Take small steps and enjoy the benefits of every change you make, and you will see that, when you change the way you live, you will not want to go back to how things were before.

And if you are scared to start because you think it's just another cost, remember that decluttering means "getting rid of";

therefore, you will not have to spend any money. You may even make a little income if you sell some things on eBay or other platforms. Sell any knick-knacks that take space and collect dust, items you never use, and clothes you don't wear. Be glad to let them go and clear your living space, your head, and your life.

Start everything with a clean canvas.

NOTES:
- Declutter!
- If things don't have a home stored away, you don't need them.
- Sell stuff you don't use.
- Simplify the way you live.
- Keep your home tidy.
- Use Fengshui tips for harmony in your living and working spaces.
- Enjoy your routines: waking up, showering, pampering yourself, eating, and sleeping.

47

NETWORKING

The previous chapters were about improving your health, image, mind, and home. If you don't feel you are a changed woman by now, go back and re-read everything!

It's essential to do this as a step-by-step project to ensure success. Read the book as you would a manual, not a novel!

The following chapters will teach you how to meet wealthy individuals and form a circle of high-calibre people. Your network will be your net worth.

Placing yourself where the rich are is paramount. But being unprepared when you meet high-calibre people would be a recipe for disaster. If you don't make the right impression, you will miss out on the opportunity to form a connection.

If you were a diligent student up to this chapter, now you should:
- be a healthy size
- have the right mindset
- possess excellent manners
- walk and move with grace

- have an impeccable image
- dress with elegance
- live in a decluttered environment

If you can tick all the boxes, you are ready to start mixing with the rich.

However:
- if your BMI says that you are overweight or underweight, go back to the "WEIGHT" chapter
- if you haven't solved the skin problem, go back to the "SKIN" chapter
- if you still dress too provocatively or your clothes are too sloppy, go back to the "CLOTHES" chapter
- if you still speak with food in your mouth, go back to the "GOOD MANNERS" chapter
- if your house is disorganised or looks like a student dorm, go back to the "YOUR HOME" chapter and learn to live like an elegant grownup
- if you still doubt this project, go back to the "MIND" chapter

You are **NOT** ready!

People tend to rush because they are curious to see what's next and rarely pay attention to what is important; this is why only a small percentage of people succeed.

But the ones of you who want this with your whole being and take the process very seriously, by now, should be entirely changed. And you are ready to build your network.

Remember that being prepared to meet prosperous people doesn't necessarily mean you will immediately meet "the one". So, for now, focus on building a network of affluent people.

Let's say that you live in the UK and decide to attend some of the significant annual events listed in the next chapter. You will see that there are annual events happening every season. If you live outside of the UK, you must find out and make a list of the annual events happening in your country and follow the same steps:

1) Pick the events that interest you and do all your research beforehand.

2) Check dates, location, costs, dress code, etiquette, transportation, accommodation (if necessary).

3) Find out how to get tickets or invitations to each event you choose. Some events are by invitation only; if you don't know

someone who can invite you, mark it as "possible" and research another one.

4) Finally, to ensure you got all the information, call the organisers - you will find all the contact details on their respective websites - and ask everything you want to know.

5) Write down the information! Having the details written down is essential so you can do your checklist before attending.

It's enough to attend one event, and if you are elegant, charming, open to meeting people and have business cards to give out, you will make new acquaintances. And then, you will undoubtedly find someone who knows someone who can get you invited to places more difficult to get into.

Do people want something in return when they do something for you? **No, they don't!** Most wealthy people are generous by nature.

And if it does happen to come across someone offensive, you can recognise their ill intentions and distance yourself from them. Always walk away from uncomfortable situations! But generally, just because a new friend may be able to get you into a place or an event, it doesn't mean they are expecting something other than a "thank you" from you. You are a grownup and should know how to filter bad people.

After you made your list of events you will be attending this year, you will have to prepare long in advance.

For example:
- If you picked Ascot, you should get a nice hat and a race day dress.
- If it's BAFTA, you must wear a full evening gown. (Remember that renting an evening gown for a formal event makes more sense when your budget is limited. Read the DRESSES chapter).
- If it's Polo, you need a smart casual outfit and NOT stilettos.
- If it's The Game Fair, country clothing would be appropriate.
Etc
- Prepare your outfits in advance and do all your research to ensure that you look and behave appropriately.
- Find reviews and pictures of the events from previous years and check out the outfits and the vibe.
- Locate the place on the map and use Google street view to familiarise yourself with the grounds as much as possible.

Being well-prepared will give you an incredible confidence boost, even in places you will attend for the first time.

Keep informed at all times!

The next decision is whether to go alone or bring someone with you. Take your time making this decision, as bringing the wrong person can be a wasted trip.

- If you are shy and feel that having someone with you will help you, consider bringing a friend. But find someone like-minded; otherwise, they can ruin your whole experience. Avoid bringing someone who drinks excessively, misbehaves, moans, or flirts shamelessly with everyone. So be very picky about whom you'll bring along.
- However, if you decide to go alone, arrive a little early and introduce yourself to a few sets of people, to have some familiar faces to return to throughout the event.

Pay attention when you meet new people:
- Memorise their names.
- Be present and listen.
- Have a light and pleasant conversation for a while, but don't

glue yourself to one person for the entire event.

- Tell them what a pleasure it was for you to meet them.
- Leave them your business cards and carry on mingling with other people.
- A good trick is using their name a few times in the conversation. They'll be very impressed, and it will help you memorise it.

If you end up conversing with two or more people simultaneously, alternate the eye contact between them, even if only one does most of the talking. Find a way to engage with all of them equally, even if it's only through the occasional smile to "the non-talking ones" or looking at them and raising your eyebrows in surprise at something that "the talking one" just said.

If you have a conversation with a couple, try to find a way to compliment the woman, even if it's indirectly ("John, you are fortunate to be accompanied by the lady with the most beautiful dress/smile here today!"). You can say this as you walk away so the compliment doesn't make them feel awkward. Instead, they'll think: "What a delightful lady!"

A beautiful and elegant woman will always make a good impression among gentlemen, but you must also make friends with the ladies. You don't want to be seen as a threat. So, be kind and pleasant to everyone!

Ideally, you would go to the lavatory and make notes (about the people you just met) on a pocket-size notebook which you will carry with you all the time. Or you can use your phone to write in your Notes folder. For example: "John & Tiggy Thompson / met at Polo / live in Surrey / come every year / she is an interior designer / we'll meet again at PAD fair."

You could add on your notes what they do for a living if you picked up on something they said - which is why paying attention is crucial! If they mention: "I helped out with the interior. I'm a designer, " you can say: "It looks fabulous; do you do many corporate events?" But if they don't mention their field, don't ask what they do for a living soon after you meet them.
The question "What do you do for a living?" is OK at corporate events, but avoid asking that immediately after meeting someone new at social events.

Learn to work the room and talk to as many people as possible, but don't do it desperately. Instead, do it in a relaxed manner and with style. Speak slowly and softly and enunciate your words. And don't be afraid to communicate if you are not native. Any foreign or regional accent can be charming if you are soft-spoken, your vocabulary is refined, and you enunciate, so that people can understand you. **Learn to beautifully speak the language of the country where you live!** If you are a native or a foreigner, consider softening a strong accent when necessary, and you should constantly improve your vocabulary.

Absorb as much information as possible about the event you are attending and make notes when you visit the lavatory, which will transfer to a journal when you are back home or to your hotel room (if you travel for the event).

Stay until the end, but don't be the last to leave.
And just before you go, try to say goodbye to the people you spoke with. It's always worth saying something like: "Have a safe journey back home, and hopefully, we'll meet again!". They'll remember you.

And then, not immediately, but ideally within 24 hours, you will send follow-up emails to the guests who shared their

business cards with you. In the subject box, put your name and where you met. And in the body of the email, sneak in a reminder to refresh their memory: it can be something that happened while you were talking, or a topic you both enjoyed discussing.
For example:
"Many thanks to John for imparting his knowledge about Polo."
or
"Here is the article we discussed."

Following up with people you liked at events will strengthen the connection and form friendships.
Networking is crucial in this process. Efficient networking will eliminate timewasters and help you build a web of lovely friends and acquaintances.

Keep your email short, don't ask for any favours, but suggest meeting for a coffee soon and ensure your details are in the email's signature. Proofread your email several times before sending it!

Your education and general knowledge are fundamental to your transformation, so always read and get informed. And every time you attend an event, make sure you learn something, even if that subject is outside your sphere of interest.

***

Let's say you picked 12 annual events you want to attend next year (in your country). You did the research in terms of etiquette, picked your outfits, and arranged accommodation for the ones which require overnight stay. You also checked the venues and photos of the previous year and learned how to network. As a result, you feel very comfortable and are looking forward to these events.

Now, you must plan for a couple of weekend breaks abroad. You shouldn't stretch yourself, so picking two destinations should be enough; choose one in the winter and one in the summer.
For example, if you live in Europe, plan:
- a weekend in Nice, in the summer
- a weekend in Gstaad, in the winter
(This is only an example. I'll leave a list of holiday destinations for the wealthy in a future chapter, and you can choose the ones you wish.)

Reserve your plane ticket and accommodation early and make the most of your weekend there. Go to the beach (if it's summer) or the slopes (if it's winter), to the restaurants, chat with people, find local events and parties and try to make as many connections as possible.

It's enough to get an invitation to one party, and you will meet people who will invite you again. And remember to maintain your dignity! You will not misbehave or gain a bad reputation! Instead, you will always remain classy, elegant, and well-mannered! Weekend flings are not acceptable! You prepare in advance and save to pay for these weekends; you cannot waste them with weekend flings. You must remain focused on what it's important. And that is networking efficiently, making a good impression and staying decent.

If you like a guy, stay in touch and form a connection to see if there is potential. You want to find out if he is a man of high standards before you allow anything physical to happen. Otherwise, you may find out that he is just a guy who sleeps around with pretty women, and you will have to bear the embarrassment when you bump into him in future, when your network expands. So, stay classy!

***

To recap:

- Pick from the list of annual events two or three events for each season. (If you live outside of the UK, find the annual events in your country, and follow the same steps)
- Find out if you need a ticket or an invitation. If it's a ticket, purchase it early. Many events are sought after, and the tickets sell fast.
- Find the locations and familiarise yourself with the grounds. Use Google Street View to get a better idea so you don't look like a lost sheep when you arrive.
- Use photos from previous years to get the vibe.
- Find out the dress code and prepare beforehand. Most events have a smart casual dress code, but if you pick one that requires a gown, don't buy it. Instead, rent it. As you learned in the DRESSES chapter, purchasing an expensive evening dress is a bad investment if you have a smaller budget.
- Decide if you are confident enough to go on your own. If you go with someone, make sure you pick the right person.
- If you go alone and it's an organised event in a smaller venue, arrive a little earlier and introduce yourself to

a few people to boost your confidence and have someone to turn to during the event.

- Have a systematic plan and approach people with grace.
- Don't retire with a drink in a corner to people-watch. Mingle and talk to a good number of people.
- Don't be afraid to take the first step and approach someone. If everyone were scared to make the first move, networking events would be obsolete.
- Memorise people's names. A good trick is to use their names a few times in conversation: "So, Lavinia, do you come to The Serpentine Summer Party every year?"
- Be present and listen. Give the person in front of you your undivided attention. This is what makes you memorable. Don't look around while you converse with someone.
- Don't talk incessantly without being considerate of the other person. Always listen more and speak less. Some experts suggest imagining a discussion as a tennis court: sometimes the ball is in your court, and sometimes the ball is in theirs.

- When you talk to someone, if you listen carefully, you may find a way to assist. They may want to attend an event, and you can put them in touch with the organisers. Perhaps they are interested in a book you have. They may need the services of an IT engineer. Focusing on giving rather than receiving will make you memorable. And people may reciprocate the gesture sometime in future. But do not over-commit and start feeling guilty about speaking again or staying in touch. If you promised to do something, do it as soon as possible. It could be an introduction, an article, a website, etc. If you said you would do it, keep your word and build trust.
- Don't criticise the event, the organiser or the people present. Don't have a negative attitude, as it's nothing more unpleasant when you first meet someone than hearing them moan or complain about something.
- Have a light and pleasant conversation for a while, but don't glue yourself to one person for the entire event.
- Don't be afraid to move to new people and conversations; do it with

class and elegance. You don't want to be perceived as rude.

- Let people know it was a pleasure meeting them, repeat their names as you leave your business cards and mingle with others.
- When you visit the lavatory, write notes about the people you met and facts you learned from the conversation. It will help with the follow-up email.
- Some of the annual events are in smaller venues where you can mingle. But other events occur outdoors or on large sites, so you can't easily approach people and introduce yourself. But in the right circumstances, conversations progress naturally. For example, let's say you are at an art fair, enjoying the art and observing the people. An exquisite lady with a smile and a pleasant demeanour will draw people to her, whether the venue is big or small. And you can end up having a friendly conversation with at least one person and exchanging business cards. Also, if you like the art of a particular gallery, ask to be added to their emailing list. This way, whenever there is a new launch, they

will invite you, which will be another networking opportunity.

- When conversing with two or more people, make eye contact with everyone. Don't look only at the person who talks and ignore those who listen.
- If you speak to a couple, find a subtle way to compliment the woman. It will be seen as a sweet gesture, and the women's friendship is essential in your elevating process.
- Never look or sound desperate! Relax and enjoy the process of making new acquaintances.
- Within 24 hours of meeting new people, send a follow-up email (or message, when appropriate) asking to meet for a coffee. Find a small thing that happened or was said at the event and mention it in the email. It will help the person remember you. Nowadays, texting or even WhatsApp-ing someone is acceptable as a follow-up. Use your judgement, though, as some prefer to keep a more formal way of communicating.
- After you have sorted your annual events, pick two weekend breaks

from the list of holiday destinations chapter.

- Choose one weekend in the summer and one in the winter.
- Purchase your plane tickets and your accommodation early.
- While on your weekend breaks, make sure you meet people and socialise. Exchange cards and stay in touch.
- When you network, go to enjoy yourself but don't get drunk and don't forget your manners! You should never get drunk anywhere, let alone in front of strangers.
- And through the networking process, stay classy!
- After each networking event, when you come home, update your spreadsheet with notes about the people you met. Initially, you wouldn't know which people are good to keep, who is a timewaster, who gives you an uncomfortable feeling and whom to put in the file "Avoid, when seeing again". So, you will have to categorise on a first impression, and then, as you meet them at various events, you will update your findings.

The best way to start your list is to put the new people you meet into three categories:
- **Timewasters** (avoid these people if you bump into them at various social functions)
- **Ambiguous** (when their nature is unclear to you, and you need more time to form an opinion about them)
- **Keepers** (you know you want them in your life)

For example:

Johnathan Riss
- met at Belgravia street party / comes from a wealthy background / drinks a lot / loud and obnoxious
(he will fall under **TIMEWASTERS**)

David Miller
- met at a gallery opening / seems fascinating / but too charming and flirtation / didn't get to speak much / we exchanged cards
(He will be under the **AMBIGUOUS** category because you couldn't quite form an opinion if you would like to stay in touch with him)

Renatta Davies
- we were introduced at Yvonne's brunch / runs a think tank on global education /

brilliant and exciting / great conversation /
we planned to meet for lunch
(She is in the **KEEPERS** category)

Eric Frost
- met first time at BAFTA / 14th Feb 2020 /
lawyer / member of Zulu Club / likes to brag
/ claims that he's friends with Debbie
Rothschild / lives in Soho
- bumped into him at ZUMA / 17th July
2020 / introduced me to Francesca Torros /
he seemed much more relaxed this time
around
(**AMBIGUOUS**)

Francesca Torros
- met first time at ZUMA / was celebrating
birthday / 17th July 2020 / introduced by
Eric Frost / IT girl / lives in Chelsea / seems
lovely / has holiday house in Brescia, Italy /
boyfriend works in banking
(**KEEPERS**)

John & Tiggy Thompson
- met at Polo / live in Surrey / come every
year / she is an interior designer / we'll meet
at PAD fair
(**KEEPERS**)

As you learn more about the people you
meet, they may change their category in
your chart. So, write notes to remember

what made you change your opinion about them. It would also be helpful to make notes not only of how you met them, but also to whom they introduced you.

It's essential to remember the face, the name and how you met a person. It gives you the upper hand when you walk up to them confidently, the next time you see them and present yourself:
"Hello, Poppy! I'm Danielle Fischer. Our friend, Ruby Sanders, introduced us at Masterpiece last year. It's lovely seeing you again!"
And the conversation starts.

Even if the person doesn't remember you, it is unlikely that they will walk away without making some small talk and perhaps exchanging business cards. So, carry business cards with you! Always!

The spreadsheet may not seem the most conventional method, but if done well, this little "database" of acquaintances can be a great networking tool. So don't dismiss it until you've tried it!

48

ANNUAL EVENTS

It's essential to educate yourself about the annual social calendar where you live and to start attending some of the events.

Research the main high society events throughout the year in the country where you live and plan to get to some of them.

Attending some of the ones happening abroad is a plus, but for now, start with the ones closest to where you live.

The events can be anything from prestigious art fairs to galas, film festivals, tennis championships, Polo, horseracing, charity balls etc.

Make a chronological list of the annual events and plan for the ones you can attend. Then, study the dress code for each of them and start working on your outfits early. If you have an extensive wardrobe and can assemble suitable outfits for each event, ensure everything is clean and set aside.

As suggested in the previous chapter, consider at least two weekend breaks a year to travel to affluent holiday destinations.

For example, in the summer, it is well known that the South of France is the desired destination for the rich. If you go for a weekend to any of the places on the French Riviera, you will meet people of high calibre, and you may be invited to future events during the same summer.

Also, in the winter, many wealthy people ski in Switzerland, France, Italy, Austria etc. So, book a weekend at any ski resorts listed in the chapter "WHERE DO THE RICH GO ON HOLIDAY".

If you live in other parts of the world, find summer and winter holiday destinations (for the wealthy) closer to you and prepare in advance, so that you can save money on tickets and accommodation.

Placing yourself where the wealthy go is paramount!

Make sure that you take advantage of all the opportunities presented to you. And always seek opportunities when you feel they don't present themselves to you.

Remember that you may not necessarily find a man in a romantic sense immediately, but you will meet people with whom you can socialise. If you like them, you will stay in touch; they can introduce you to other people, and your network will expand.

And you don't have to make substantial financial sacrifices to meet rich people. You just need to learn to plan and strategise correctly.

Some of the significant annual events happening in the UK are listed below. Of course, there are many more, but start with these, and you will learn the full social calendar as you go along:

- The Mayfair Antique & Fine Art Fair - January
- British Academy of Film and Television Arts (BAFTA) - February
- London Fashion Week - February
- Cheltenham Gold Cup - March
- The Grand National - April
- Oxford/Cambridge Boat Race - April
- The London Yacht, Jet & Prestige Car Show - April
- The Badminton Horse Trials - April/May
- The Derby - June
- Royal Ascot - June

- Royal Windsor Horse Show - May
- British Motor Show - May
- Glyndebourne - May-August
- Royal Windsor Horse Show - Spring - Summer
- Royal Ascot - June
- Boodles Tennis - June
- Hay Festival May - June
- Cartier Queen's Cup May - June
- Chelsea Flower Show - May - June
- Eton Fourth of June - June
- Investec Derby - June
- Hurlingham Fête - June
- Queen's Club Championships - June
- Royal Academy Summer Party - June
- The Victoria & Albert Museum Summer Party - June
- Trooping the Colour - June
- Chestertons Polo in the Park - June
- Royal Ascot - June
- The Serpentine Party - June
- Opera Holland Park - June - August
- Henley Royal Regatta June - July
- Wimbledon Lawn Tennis Championship - June - July
- Goodwood Festival of Speed - June / July
- Grange Park Opera, Surrey Hills - June - July
- Garsington Opera at Wormsley - June - July

- The Grange Festival, Hampshire - June - July
- Masterpiece London - June - July
- Nevill Holt Opera - June - July
- The Spectator Summer Party - July
- Moët & Chandon July Festival at Newmarket - July
- King Power Gold Cup - July
- Goodwood Festival - July
- Peterborough Royal Foxhound Show - July
- The Game Fair - July
- Womad Festival - July
- Royal Henley Regatta - July
- The British Grand Prix (Formula 1) - July - August
- Cowes Week - July - August
- Wilderness Festival - August
- Burghley Horse Trials - August - September
- Salon Privé - August - September
- Goodwood Revival - September
- LAPADA Art & Antiques Fair - September
- London Fashion Week - September
- PAD London Art + Design Fair - October
- Frieze London and Frieze Masters - October
- King George VI Chase – December

49

WHERE DO THE RICH GO ON HOLIDAY

Some of the holiday destinations for the rich are:

- Amalfi Coast
- Antibes
- Aruba
- Aspen
- Avignon
- Azores
- Bali
- Barbados
- Barcelona
- Bath
- Beaulieu-sur-Mer
- Bora Bora
- Cabo San Lucas
- Cannes
- Cape Cod
- Cape Town
- Capri
- Cortina d'Ampezzo
- Courchevel
- Cinque Terre
- Dingle
- Dubai
- Dubrovnik
- Fiji

- Florence
- Geneva
- Gstaad
- Ibiza
- Jackson Hole
- Lake Como
- Lake Tahoe
- Las Vegas
- Laucala Island
- London
- Los Cabos
- Lyon
- Maldives
- Mallorca
- Marbella
- Maui
- Megève
- Milan
- Monaco
- Monte Carlo
- Mykonos
- Nantucket
- Necker Island
- Nice
- Palm Beach
- Paris
- Portofino
- Positano
- Punta Cana
- Rome
- St Barths
- Seychelles

- St Jean Cap Ferrat
- St Kitts
- St Lucia
- St Moritz
- St Tropez
- The Hamptons
- Tuscany
- Vail
- Val-d'Isère
- Venice
- Verbier
- Villefranche-sur-Mer
- Whistler
- Windsor
- Zermatt
- Zurich

~ 50 ~

FOOD

A healthy diet is essential for nutrition and good health.

But while working on this project, not only must you be sensible with what you eat, but you should also be careful WHEN you eat certain foods.

For example, 24 hours before you go networking, you should avoid garlic, onion, curry, and other similar foods producing unpleasant odours that will stay in your body for many hours. Sometimes the smell of pungent foods seeps through your pores, so NEVER have such foods if you are due to go to a function or a date. If you crave strong-smelling foods, have them at home and stay away from people for 24 hours.

Just because you brushed your teeth, flossed, and had a shower doesn't necessarily change the odour that your body eliminates after eating certain foods. Trust me that these smells can make people feel sick. I've been near people after they had pungent food, and being in their vicinity wasn't easy.
You don't want to overwhelm people around you by wearing strong perfume or by exuding any unpleasant odours.

Generally, keep your diet as healthy as possible, consuming mainly vegetables, fruit, nuts, and fish, and keep the consumption of meat and dairy at a minimum.

Have food intolerance & allergy testing and be gentle with what you consume.

Drink plenty of water and learn about fasting. Giving your body a break from food, occasionally, can be beneficial. Do your research before fasting to see what works for you and speak to a nutritionist for thorough advice. Don't fast if your doctor tells you no to, but don't dismiss fasting without researching it. It's a great way to lose weight if done correctly and in conjunction with a healthy lifestyle. But always use the advice of specialists before making any significant changes to your diet.

What you eat and drink will impact your physical and mental health. Getting proper nutrition helps with the ageing process for your mind and body. And if in the previous chapters you learned how to handle yourself with grace, you must learn to treat the inside of your body with grace too. Listen to your body to understand what it can tolerate and what upsets it and be gentle with it so you can age gracefully.

Get regular check-ups and annual blood tests and correct any deficiencies with vitamin and mineral supplements suggested by doctors and nutritionists.

NOTES:

- Keep a healthy diet of vegetables, fruit, seeds, nuts, fish and very little meat and dairy
- Test yourself for food intolerances and allergies
- Have regular check-ups with specialists and correct any vitamin and mineral deficiencies
- And don't eat smelly foods 24 hours before meeting people

~ 51 ~

DRINKS

Water is the only drink that your body needs.

With any other beverages, you must be selective if you consume them regularly.

Alcohol
If you used to drink beer, cider, and soft drinks in the past, now you should remove them from your drinks list.

If you spoil yourself with an alcoholic beverage occasionally, make your experience more enjoyable by having a more sophisticated drink than beer and cider. Alcohol is not a necessity for one's life, so if you treat yourself, have something more refined, such as champagne, a good wine, a cocktail etc.

If you dine with people, have a glass or two of wine. But if you eat on your own, stick with water to give your system a break.

Occasionally, when you are out and with pleasant company, spoil yourself and have a little champagne, an aperitif, a cocktail, a brandy, a cognac etc. But never drink more than you can handle! A drunk woman will not attract a man with high standards. On the contrary, she will probably attract another drunk.

Drink alcohol in moderation and stay under the recommended number of units! Be gentle with your body!

Juices
Regarding juices, be careful with how natural they are and how often you consume them. Vegetable juices are better than fruit juices but speak to a nutritionist or research if you want to introduce more fresh juices into your diet.

Teas

Introduce herbal teas into your daily routine. Buy them organic and experiment with different varieties. Drink them hot or cold, and best unsweetened.

Coffee
Drink coffee in moderation.

Water
Stay hydrated through the day by drinking plenty of water! Drinking enough water helps with weight control, digestive regularity, physical performance, brain function, energy and mood, better skin etc.

NOTES:
- NEVER GET DRUNK!
- Stop drinking beer, cider, and soft drinks.
- The more refined alcoholic beverages are champagne, wine, cocktails, brandy, cognac etc.
- Treat alcohol as a treat and have it less.
- Fruit juices can be calorie bombs, so drink less.
- Vegetable juices are healthy and may contain fewer calories.
- Experiment with herbal teas and introduce them into your daily diet but drink them unsweetened.
- Have coffee in moderation.

- Drink plenty of water!

~ 52 ~

HOW TO HOLD THE GLASS WHEN DRINKING WINE AND CHAMPAGNE

- Pinch the stem of the glass with your thumb, index and middle fingers.
- Hold the glass by the middle of the stem or lower towards the base.
- Never touch the bowl; it will change the drink's temperature and leave unsightly stains.
- Tilt your wrist slightly for each sip.
- Drink from the same side to avoid leaving lipstick or lip-gloss marks all over the glass.
- Don't lift your pinky!

Some people mistakenly think lifting your finger is a fancy way of drinking. On the contrary, it is believed that the habit may come from France. According to William Hanson, a British etiquette expert: "before the Revolution, there was quite a lot of promiscuity amongst the upper classes. And when you were at Court and drinking tea, you would extend your little finger to show that you had a sexually transmitted disease, so if anyone was going to make a move on you, they knew beforehand. It was considered good etiquette to let people know, so someone who would lift their finger would take an interest in someone else who lifted their finger, rather than someone who didn't." (William Hanson)

So, next time you want to lift your finger when drinking something, remember that little story and keep the pinky down because it is neither elegant nor classy, and the etiquette experts are appalled by this gesture!

The ones listed above are the most basic rules that everyone should know. It's painful seeing people holding a glass of wine or champagne by the bowl. But if you would like to learn more about how to keep, open, pour and enjoy wine and champagne, go to a wine-tasting course or research online, as there is plenty of material.

For now, ensure that you are holding the glass correctly. And as you learned in the GOOD MANNERS chapter, never point out someone's mistakes if you see them holding the glass incorrectly. Instead, always focus on how **YOU** do things while learning from others.

~ 53 ~

SMOKING

If you smoke, stop! If you don't smoke, never start!

Smoking is a vile and unhealthy habit, and everyone who was unwise to start it during adolescence should, at least, give it up when they reach proper adulthood.

If you are in your thirties and still smoke, you are putting yourself at significant risk with every passing year. The graphic pictures on the cigarette packs are there for a reason; therefore, going into detail about the harmful effects of smoking is unnecessary.

Smoking causes tremendous damage, so if the pictures on the cigarette pack don't convince you, research it and give up immediately.

Adopt any method that may help you and try as many times as necessary until you give up. There is nothing good about smoking. And your health is the most important.

Also, when you want to meet a high-value man, you must know that if they don't smoke themselves, most rich men don't like women who smoke.

The clothes and hair smell, and rarely will you meet a nonsmoker accepting this habit from their partner. Usually, affluent people find smoking ghastly!

If you are in the process of giving up and you think that you have cravings occasionally, try this exercise:
- take deep breaths as if you were smoking, but without the cigarette
- take 10, 20, 30 deep breaths and then drink water
- do that throughout the day, but never reach for the cigarette

This exercise relaxes you, and you will not need to reach for the cigarette.

Sometimes you may be invited to a beautiful cigar bar, and having a cigar with your cognac is not seen as unclassy. If anything, a woman smoking a cigar can look stylish, but only if it's done **occasionally** and in the proper settings.

But not cigarettes!

Being addicted to smoking cigarettes is not elegant.
Give up immediately!

~ 54 ~

HOW TO CONVERSE

LISTEN ATTENTIVELY
A great conversationalist is a person who knows how to listen before anything else. Being present, paying attention and understanding what is being discussed is a sign of intelligence, and you show respect to the people with whom you interact by listening to them.

DON'T INTERRUPT
Don't rush to speak over people! It's infuriating for others if you do this!

Let them finish what they are saying, and then, you talk. Should you need to add something urgently, wait until the person completes their thought before you start talking.

You are an excellent communicator if you make others feel important by allowing them to be heard.

ASK QUESTIONS

Just listening to someone impassively is not enough. Instead, you must engage with the person who speaks by asking them questions about the discussed topic.

If someone finishes what they say and then it's an awkward silence, they may feel that their story wasn't exciting enough. So, ask questions to indicate that you were listening and would like to know more.

But only ask questions to which you genuinely want to know the answers. Don't be the one who asks questions loudly just to attract other people's attention. People experienced in networking (and most elite people **are** experienced) can identify a phoney who asks questions to look smart to others.

While intelligence is appreciated, conceitedness is not! So, ask questions only if genuinely interested; otherwise, excuse yourself and mingle with others in the room.

BE CONFIDENT BUT RESPECTFUL!

Don't confuse confidence with arrogance!
Always be polite!
And always treat everyone with respect!

Remember that elegance is about how you make others feel around you. Don't be afraid to lead a conversation but do it gently; don't dominate it. Talk in a manner that draws people in, and they feel compelled by what you say.

READ, LISTEN, LEARN
Keep an open mind and learn about every subject so you never feel like you don't belong.
Keep up to date with current news and events and expand your sphere of interest to gain more knowledge.

And if you only know little about something, ask the person who knows more to share their wisdom with you. Even doing this makes you a great communicator.

DON'T BE CONTROVERSIAL
Be careful about what subjects you decide to discuss. For example, avoid discussing politics, as you don't want to have a heated debate with someone.

Of course, if a person at a gathering makes a light remark such as: "The traffic was bad due to the protest outside of Parliament.", you don't need to shut them down with a categoric "I don't want to discuss politics!". After all, the statement was mainly about heavy traffic. You don't even know if it would have been an extended topic. So instead, you can say: "Hopefully, the protest will finish by the time you return home, so you won't have to get stuck in traffic again". This way, you have a light, thoughtful, pleasant conversation.

If you see that the person would want to extend on the topic of the protest (which may be current news with very divided opinion), you can divert the subject towards a less controversial topic.

If you divert the subject by asking a question, it will be a smart choice, as the person will want to answer. And if the question is something about them, it will be even smarter as you get them to talk about themselves, and most people like talking about themselves.

Topics never to discuss while networking:
- Politics
- Religion
- Race
- Ethnicity
- Gender
- Health
- Views on the pandemic
- Money
- Sex

Choose pleasant topics and maintain the conversation light and enjoyable.

BREATHE CORRECTLY
If you control your breath while you talk, your speech will be smooth and flow nicely. You will never run out of breath, and you will never end up speaking in a squeaky voice. The tone must be kept constant and pleasant.

Many people hold their breath when they speak, which is wrong.
One should speak while exhaling.

Try this exercise:
- breathe in through your nose before saying something
- then read a long sentence as you breathe out through your mouth

You will see that you have better control over your voice and sound more articulate.

If you take gasps of air through your mouth while you speak, it will dry out your throat, and your voice will sound hoarse.
Breathing in through your nose will filter and humidify the air which goes in. Your mouth is not designed to do that. Breathing through your mouth will give you a sore

throat and make your voice sounds breathy, raspy, or strained.

So, always breathe in (through your nose) before speaking and let out the breath steadily while you say words.

CONTROL YOUR SPEED
Speaking too fast is a sign of nervousness or a lack of self-esteem.

Some famous speakers can deliver a great speech at a fast pace, but that usually happens after they have had voice training to speak on stage to large audiences. And everything is well-studied and rehearsed so they can keep the listeners captivated. They deliver their thoughts fast because it's a speech, not a conversation.

However, in conversation, where two or more people are involved, there needs to be a nice flow for the experience to be positive and for people to remember you as charming.

If you are surrounded by family and friends who speak fast, you tend to adopt the same habit. So, hire an elocution coach to improve how you talk or find material (books and videos) that can help you.

Record yourself reading, identify the best-sounding pace, and try to keep that speed always.
At first, you won't remember to do it all the time.
Sometimes, you may start with the right speed and then increase it without realising it.
So, start reading and recording yourself regularly, and you will be able to control the speed.

SPEAK SOFTLY
Don't be loud when you speak!
But also, don't be meek and mousy!
Find the right balance to not fall into any extremes.
Learn to be gentle in your speech but decisive and articulate.

A feminine voice is about delivering your words eloquently but with finesse and without sounding aggressive or angry.

ELEVATE YOUR VOCABULARY
- Read classic novels and listen to radio channels where they discuss books, arts and culture to help elevate your vocabulary.
- Speak your language correctly and enunciate your words.

- Don't be concerned with any accent you may have. Instead, work to soften it and make your speech clear. Your accent will be delightful if you enunciate and have a gentle tone of voice.
- Mind your grammar and your pronunciation, and never swear! In any language!
- Don't use slang! Speak the standard language and master your grammar.

Many successful people had to practice through appropriate training and practice. It can take three weeks to several months, but you can form any habit. So, start working towards making the way you speak a remarkable character trait.

Mastering the art of conversing is a powerful skill, and you can win anyone with it. But, on the other hand, a beautiful woman who cannot speak well or has an unpleasant voice is like a beautiful-looking cake with a dry and disappointing filling.

NOTES:
- Listen more and speak less
- Don't interrupt
- Ask questions and be genuinely interested
- Stay away from controversial topics

- Expand your vocabulary
- Master your grammar
- Control your breathing
- Speak slowly and softly
- Enunciate

~ 55 ~

FACIAL EXPRESSIONS

Frowning or having a constant stern face is associated with negative emotions. Some people do it involuntarily, making themselves (probably unintentionally) unapproachable. So, don't adopt a severe look if you don't feel sad about something. Instead, relax your face and have a friendly expression all the time. A constant stern look takes away from one's attractiveness. And frowning will give the impression that one doesn't want to be approached.

So, unless you attend a sombre event, never keep a constant sad face.

Read about the "Duchenne smile", the technique that teaches you how to "smile with your eyes". Then watch videos on how to do it properly and remember to use the smile throughout the day.

The method is relatively straightforward, and almost everyone knows how to smile with their eyes, but only a few people remember to do it daily.

A fake smile doesn't reach the eyes. Instead, it stays on the lower face, lifting the corners of your mouth (and possibly the cheeks) but not the corners of your eyes.

A Duchenne smile lifts the corners of your mouth, your cheeks and the corners of your eyes. A smile which reaches your eyes is associated with pure enjoyment and makes one more approachable and trustworthy.

To understand the effectiveness of a genuine smile, do this exercise in the mirror:

- Put your palms in front of your face, covering your mouth, nose and cheeks, leaving only the eyes uncovered. Next, lift the corners of your mouth into a fake smile and watch your eyes. Nothing will change.

- Now, with your face covered and only your eyes showing, recall and relive one of the happiest events of your life and allow your face to smile naturally. You will notice that your eyes will change shape, and you will get a little twinkle, making them sparkle. That is the "Duchenne smile". Learn it and practice it to brighten your face all the time.

If you get used to smiling with your eyes (even when alone), it will become second nature. The more you do it, the quicker you remember to smile when your face goes stern.

A well-executed "Duchenne smile" will light up your face, make your eyes sparkle, and turn you irresistible!

When you talk or listen to someone, and the subject is sad, it's natural to show compassion or sorrow, but if you are happy, let your face show it!

An expression which should not show on an elegant woman's face is the expression of disgust. You don't need to relay events or stories which may create disgust. And if someone else tells you an unpleasant story, it would be much better to say something to show compassion, surprise, and solidarity than distort your face in repulsion. I don't know anyone whose face looked beautiful while displaying feelings of disgust or contempt.

Maybe you can say: "I'm sorry that you had to experience such things!" or "That is terrible!" or "I sympathise with you!". But don't grimace or distort your face in a way that would make you unattractive.

When something is amusing, it's appropriate to have a good laugh, but the laughter must be genuine and caused by something that happened at that moment. Plastering a continuous large grin on your face makes you look insincere.

Use the appropriate facial expressions to make yourself pleasant and open to communication.

And some tips to remember how to smile genuinely:

- Being in love makes you look luminous.
- Gratitude for things that you have makes your face look soft and gentle.
- So be in love with your life and be grateful for everything and everyone you know; those feelings will give you the inner joy that will make you smile with your eyes.

WHAT YOU READ

Introduce these three things in your daily routine:
1. Keep up to date with the current news.
2. Check the daily weather where you are (or when you leave the house, to be dressed appropriately).
3. Read with the intention of learning something new every day.

***

1. Keeping up with the news doesn't necessarily mean knowing all the details of every event worldwide. Instead, inform yourself sufficiently to understand what happens in your country and be aware of the significant events globally.

2. Checking the daily weather forecast before you leave the house (especially if you live somewhere where the weather changes constantly) is essential to dress appropriately. It's a small detail; some may think anyone does that. Well, not everyone does it, and very often, you find someone

acting surprised about how hot or cold the weather is because they didn't check.

It's not elegant to sweat intensively or shiver uncontrollably. So, check the weather forecast before leaving somewhere and dress appropriately. You can be beautifully dressed, but if you seem uncomfortable (either because you are too hot, too cold, or your shoes are tight etc.), you will NOT look elegant! So, make sure you check the weather forecast before leaving the house!

3. To learn something new every day:
- Read business books so you can gain a decent financial education.
- Read classics and poetry to elevate your vocabulary.
- Read works of great philosophers for intellectual stimulation.
- Read about psychology to understand human nature.
- Re-read your history books to refresh your memory about important events that happened in the past.
- Keep a map on the wall to familiarise yourself with the geography of your country and the planet; for general knowledge, place pins with interesting facts about places that interest you.

- Read self-improvement books to discover and better yourself.
- Read and learn how to meditate and become mindful, so you can let go of blockages and ideas which may keep you from growing.
- Practice gratitude and generosity, even when you do not have much to give. Sometimes, all someone needs may be a smile. And you can easily give that!
- Keep a guide for good manners on your coffee table and apply those rules in your everyday life.

If you have gossip magazines in the house, recycle them immediately and never again buy such material! No one improved their intellect from gossip magazines!

Your transformation will not be only physical. It will be intellectual as well. And what you read and what you watch will influence you greatly. So read only from the categories listed above for a while to use your time wisely.

***

Make the above list your "curriculum" from which you continue your education.

You will be unstoppable when you realise the power that knowledge brings you!

Rich men are fascinated by intelligent women, and the way through a rich man's heart is not through his stomach, as you've probably heard your grandmother telling you about men. Instead, it's through intelligence, elegance and beauty that goes deeper than the physical aspect.

So, use your time wisely to learn the relevant skills. Of course, it's nice to be able to put a meal together, but if you aspire to win the interest and heart of a rich man, you need different attributes.

Because for a rich man, great food is easily attainable: if he doesn't want to cook, he can eat in the best restaurants or hire someone to cook his meals. But meeting a beautiful woman who is intelligent, funny, kind and exudes elegance through every pore is the ultimate prize he will want to win. (Don't get hung up on the term "prize"; it's only a metaphor!)

If you possess such attributes, any man will be intrigued and want to know you better. Provided he's single, of course! Never seduce or allow yourself to be seduced by a married man or a man in a relationship!

There is nothing elegant or classy about that!

~ 57 ~

WHO PAYS THE BILL?

This subject has been discussed to saturation, and everyone has different rules.

I guide myself by the following four scenarios:

1: Romantic dinner with a man

If a man and a woman are on a romantic date, usually, the man pays the bill. It's nothing to do with extreme masculinity, lack of feminism, or any other issue. It's just a matter of elegance.

Embarking on this project, you will be dating men with high incomes, and to them, picking up the bill is not unusual. A gentleman making millions doesn't expect you to pay the bill when you are on a date, even if you are a high earner yourself.

If in the past you had situations when you insisted on paying a restaurant bill after a date, this is something you will never do again. Refrain from insisting on paying the bill, as it would not make the best impression, and a gentleman wouldn't find this gesture feminine and elegant.

So, if you are on a date with a rich guy, don't even think about trying to pick up the bill. In most top-class restaurants, the bill is placed in front of the man anyway.

Don't stretch your neck to see how much the bill is!
Don't ask how much the bill is!
Don't ask if you should contribute to the bill!
Don't insist on paying the bill!
It's not elegant!

After the man pays the bill, you smile and thank him kindly for a wonderful meal and delightful company!

2: Dinner with friends who earn around the same as you

When dining with friends (who earn about the same as you), guide yourself by the following rules:

- When **you invite** the person, **you pay.**

- When **you suggest** dinner, you should either **take turns** (you pay this time, and your friend takes care of your next outing together), **or** you can **split the bill.**

Remember to differentiate between suggesting and inviting.
Suggesting sounds like: "Shall we meet for dinner?"
Inviting sounds like: "I would like to take you out for dinner."

- If it's dinner with **many friends** at once and **no one is hosting** the event, then you can **all split the bill.**

- If it's dinner with **many friends**, but **a host organised and invited** you, then **the host pays the bill.**

Over the years, you learn about the financial situation of your friends (even if this is not discussed in detail), and you have a general idea about where they stand on the earning scale.

So, when you go out with a friend who earns around the same amount, good etiquette would be to alternate the bill paying or to split.

If you notice that, although you earn about the same as your friend, you are always the one paying when you go out together, this is not a genuine friend, and you should limit the time you spend with them. If it bothers you terribly and you don't want to lose this friend, you can mention it gently, and they'll get the message for next time. But if the situation repeats itself, having friends who take advantage of your generosity is not worth it.

3: Dinner with friends who earn much less than you

If you are dining with a friend who earns much less than you:
- When **you invite** the person, **you pay**
- When **you suggest** dinner, **you pay**
- When **they suggest** dinner, **you pay** (if it doesn't bother you)
- When **they suggest** dinner **and insist beforehand**, "I would like to treat you this time", **they pay**

It is essential to make people feel at ease around you. If you have friends who earn less than you, treating them is elegant. But you must remember to limit your time spent with them.

You love your friends but must reserve most of your spare time to grow professionally, socially, etc.

So, occasionally, see friends who earn less than you, treat them to dinner, but be graceful and never make them feel bad. And if sometimes, they insist on treating you, accept graciously. However, don't have the most expensive item on the menu when they pay, just as you shouldn't go for the cheapest thing on the menu, because the gesture would look patronising. Especially if they know you and are certain you'd never order that in normal circumstances. Always, be considerate!

4: Non-romantic dinner with a wealthy male (or female) friend

If you are dining with a male friend who is rich and he insists on paying every time, you accept graciously; and now and then, offer to take him out.

Even if they will not let you pay, it's nice for them to feel appreciated. It's common for a wealthy person to pick up the bill every time, just as you do with people who earn less than you.

The same rule applies if your wealthy friend insisting on paying all the time is female. Occasionally, offer to do it, so she can see that you appreciate her company, not her wallet.

As mentioned above, the custom of wealthy people picking up the bill for their friends is common. So don't think their generosity is suspicious, but don't take advantage of it and always remain gracious!

~ 58 ~

THANK YOU NOTES

Send people "thank you" notes/messages after attending their dinner or being taken out for dinner.

Formal dinner:

If it was a formal dinner, send a "thank you" card or note by post, expressing your appreciation to the host for their hospitality and the delicious food. Even if you didn't think the food was tasty, it is graceful to find something nice to say and express gratitude for their time and effort.

Saying "thank you" for dinner is a sweet gesture. However, elaborating your message and making it a little more personal (by adding some enjoyable details of the evening) makes you charming. Never write something negative about the food, the evening, the host, the house, or the other guests. Even in the unlikely event that everything was terrible, you can still think of something nice to show gratitude.

If the food was not tasty, mention something about a creative dish or excellent wine. If some of the dinner guests were not to your liking, praise the host's ability to bring together such an interesting mix of people with fascinating views.

It's not advisable to lie, but you can use your imagination to find something good about the occasion to write in your "thank you" note and post it.

Nowadays, people consider even email an appropriate "thank you" note. However, when it comes to formal dinners, I prefer "thank you" notes sent via post.

Not sending a "thank you" note will be seen as rude, and there is a chance that you may not be invited again.

Dinner with a close friend:

If it was a dinner with a close friend, always send a text on the night, to thank them for the evening and to let them know that you got home safely (if you left their place) or to ask about their safe arrival home (if you dined at a restaurant).

The next day, by mid-morning, send another text, to remind them how much you enjoyed spending time with them.

- If dinner was at their home, make it personal by mentioning details you liked.
- If dinner was at the restaurant and they paid, you can thank them for the meal, for their generosity and company.
- If dinner was out and you paid, thank them for making time to see you.

An elegant woman is equally elegant if she gives or if she receives and she is equally elegant with everyone: close friends, acquaintances, and strangers.

If elegance is not constant, it is not elegance.

WHERE DO YOU FIND RICH MEN?

In the previous chapters, you found out where the rich go on holiday and the annual events they attend. Now it's time to see where they spend the rest of the time.

Generally, rich men work in the business district and live in affluent areas.

Where they work
From Monday to Friday, you are more likely to bump into them in the business district during office hours. Usually, everyone is rushing in the morning, but during lunch and after office hours, many successful professionals start frequenting restaurants, bars and hotel lounges.

In every major city, there are:
- areas where you find people who work in finance
- areas where you find law offices
- areas with private practices, where you can find wealthy people working in the medical field
- etc.

So, learn about the city where you live and, on some days, take your lunch in the financial district. On other days, go where the lawyers hang out. Other times, lunch in the areas where surgeons and medical consultants have lunch. Meet people from different industries. It's a good networking strategy.

Never go anywhere intending to pick up men! You are not a woman of ill repute! Instead, observe the vibe and do a bit of people-watching. The more you learn about affluent people, the easier it will be for you to network.

In any country, all the large cities have areas where a certain industry predominates and they are usually in the city centre.

If you live in a smaller town or village, research the nearby largest city and explore it.

Apply the same rules: find out where the affluent people work and live, make notes and plan to frequent the places to familiarise yourself with them and to observe. Learn these places by heart and spend time there whenever you can.

If you have followed the previous chapters and have the right image and attitude, people will be drawn to you, so you don't need to fear starting a conversation with strangers. Conversations will happen naturally.

But remember to remain classy and dignified! If someone approaches you with an indecent proposal, you decline and leave! Never put yourself in unpleasant and uncomfortable situations!

Generally, if you are adequately dressed and have the right attitude, people will not be offensive towards you. Of course, I'm not saying you will never meet an ill-intentioned rich man. Of course, you may come across some bad ones. But GENERALLY, you will attract well-mannered people if you look graceful and behave with elegance and decency.

You are an elevated woman now and must place yourself among the rich. Otherwise, you will never get the chance to meet them.

If you are not yet the right size to start the process, prioritise your weight and lose the extra kilos (or gain the extra kilos needed, as the case may be) to look healthy. It may seem superficial, but wealthy men have high standards and prefer healthy-looking women who are not overweight or underweight.

However, if you are satisfied with your life and weight, you do not need to concern yourself with what this book says. Enjoy your life and be happy!

But if you want to elevate yourself, get in shape first! Don't start networking with affluent people thinking that it doesn't matter that you are a size 20 now because you will lose the extra weight as you go along. If you are serious about this project, don't rush the process! Do it right: study every step and make the necessary changes to become your optimal self.

Let's say you have a few days available and would like to explore the vibe in the financial district. Have a coffee in the lounge of a hotel and watch the people going by. Or have lunch and ask for a corner table to have a good view of the restaurant plan. Watch and learn from: people's gestures (good and bad), the way they dress, the way they talk, what they eat and drink etc. Watch both men and women, not necessarily to copy them entirely but to observe the gestures that make them look gracious and those that don't. You learn a lot from watching.

By observing good and bad traits in others, you will see how people's actions reflect on them and help you determine what individual you would like to be. And always focus on your changes and bettering yourself, and the right people will come.

Where they live and "play"
Late in the evening and during weekends, you'll find the rich in affluent residential parts of town. Have your weekend coffee in these areas. Find out about the local farmer's markets, antique markets, sports clubs, luxury department stores, art galleries etc. Make a list and start frequenting these places. Private members' clubs are a great place to meet wealthy people too, but I don't advise you to rush to get a membership there because they are expensive and have a waiting list.

However, make a list of the private members' clubs in your city and check their websites for public events that you can attend without being a member.

And when your network expands, you will have friends and acquaintances who belong to private clubs, and you can ask them politely to let you know if they ever attend the events at the club to think of you as a "plus one". If you are courteous, people will happily bring you as their guest.

On many occasions, rich people are members of private clubs and are not necessarily interested in the events; they go there for business meetings, eating, or socialising.

And often, the same members belong to various private clubs, because being part of the elite circle is a status symbol for them and a networking tool.

When you make friends in that circle, ask them to tell you about the club events, as they are usually excellent. The events can be art and culture or discussions with social topics etc. Broaden your knowledge, and you will broaden your horizon.

If you are smart and have a plan, you don't have to break the bank to frequent affluent areas, but you cannot do it without money. So, as I mentioned in the first chapters, you need to have a decent income and spend your time and money wisely. Therefore, if you have a free Saturday, rather than spending it in a club with unsuccessful friends, go and have tea and a slice of cake in an upmarket hotel and enjoy the surroundings, observe the people, and make notes of the things you like.

Ideally, at some point, you would move to an affluent area. You may not be able to do it immediately but consider moving sometime in the future. Of course, it will be more expensive, you may have to downsize, and you may even need to live in a studio or share a flat with someone else, but it would benefit you immensely.

You must place yourself where the opportunities are!

LUXURY DEPARTMENT STORES
Suppose you browse the men's or electronic departments, furniture or sports or luggage departments, or even in the food hall; you can bump into single men. Of course, you don't necessarily have to go there with that sole intention, but if you find yourself there, be aware of your surroundings. You never know how you may spot someone admiring you.

LOCAL PARKS
When the park is in an affluent neighbourhood, almost anyone jogging or walking their dog lives nearby. So, if you sit on a bench and someone with a dog walks by, and the dog stops, ask if you can pet it.

Pet owners love talking about their pets. But always read people! Don't stop them if you see them in a hurry or not intending to stop.

Also, since you are not there to pick up men, don't be afraid to speak to women, too, if the dog stops in front of you and the owner seems friendly. You never know where the conversation will take you and what friendship may form in future.

Just be natural, and don't sound desperate! You are an elegant woman who makes others feel comfortable.

LOUNGES OF EXPENSIVE HOTELS
Instead of drinking coffee or tea in a coffee shop, where the music is loud, and all the clients are college students, have your coffee in the lounge of an upmarket hotel in an affluent area.

The atmosphere and coffee are better, and you can be sure that the people there are either staying in the hotel and relaxing in the lounge or having a business meeting.

However, be careful not to look desperate or to give the impression that you are there to be picked up! Be dressed as you belong, behave as you belong, and if someone approaches you to talk to you, remain classy and composed. Even if the man is handsome and you sense that there is chemistry, you must stay composed!

The most you can do is exchange business cards as you say goodbye. It doesn't matter how good-looking the man is; don't try to seduce someone immediately after you meet him.

If you like him, you can follow up and meet for a drink some other day but don't do anything in haste. Instead, think long-term and think about keeping a good reputation.

On the other hand, if you are approached by a man making the wrong assumptions, wish them a good day and leave! That will embarrass him, and you will maintain your dignity.

FARMER'S MARKETS
These little markets take place once a week (mainly at weekends), and they are usually located in little local green spaces or along a side road, surrounded by coffee shops and restaurants.

Locals in wealthy areas love to visit farmers' markets, so have your coffee at one of the coffee shops nearby and watch the buzz. It is an enjoyable pastime, and it's almost impossible not to get someone to start a conversation with you.

The little farmers' markets have such a great community feel and are delightful.

STREET PARTIES

Street parties usually happen in the summer, and they take place outdoors on a side street closed for the day. Neighbours come to socialise in a very informal, fun way, with food, drinks and live music and other forms of entertainment. There can be between 200 and 1,000 guests, and street parties in well-to-do neighbourhoods will have celebrities and wealthy locals attending. It's a great way to meet new people.

OPERA AND THEATRE IN THE GARDEN

Affluent areas have garden squares (also known as communal gardens), which are securely gated and accessed only by residents around the square.

Sometimes, the gardens host theatre productions and operas, and you can buy a ticket at a small price. Such events are rare, and the tickets get sold out fast, so ideally, sign up for the local garden square newsletter and keep an eye out for future events.

They are great occasions to mix with the locals.

ART GALLERIES
By spending a few hours, once a week, visiting art galleries, you will not only learn about art, but you can leave your details with the gallery staff to send you invitations for future events.

And while you are in the gallery, you never know; you may bump into a millionaire art lover who, by chance, happens to be there searching for a piece for his living room! So, you must place yourself in favourable places for opportunities to appear in your life!

SUMMER BARBEQUES IN GARDEN SQUARES
Some exclusive garden squares host annual barbeques for residents and their guests. Those barbeques are NOT your run-of-the-mill barbeques. They are very fashionable events, an elegant dress code is usually required, and they are packed with rich individuals. So, find out where these events are in your city and purchase a ticket early or get invited. They are great for networking!

CHURCHES AND PLACES OF WORSHIP

You may be surprised to find out that, besides the various religious celebrations throughout the year, many places of worship hold classical music concerts with tickets sold at very reasonable prices.

They'll send a seasonal schedule with their shows and other social and cultural events if you subscribe to their newsletter. The acoustics are fabulous, and the intermission is an excellent opportunity to have a glass of wine and mingle with the locals.

AT YOUR FRIENDS' FAMILY GATHERINGS

Expanding your network also means invitations to your friends' events: weddings, baptisms, christenings, Bar mitzvahs, graduations, and other private events.

You will meet single men at your new friends' family gatherings, so don't refuse such invitations.

ANTIQUE AND ART FAIRS

The antique and art fairs happen annually (as you saw in the "ANNUAL EVENTS" chapter) or as one-off occasions. Attend whenever you can because rich people are great lovers of art.

FINE DINING RESTAURANTS

Many people feel awkward eating alone in a restaurant, but if you are confident and graceful, it could be an excellent opportunity to meet people.

Remember your table manners, look relaxed and comfortable being there, and a gentleman may be intrigued to know you. So, consider dining on your own occasionally, as long as it's an upmarket restaurant.

GYMS AND HEALTH CLUBS
If you don't live yet in an affluent area but want to check out the local health club, call the reception and ask for a viewing and a couple of free passes. You can say that you want to move to the area and are considering becoming a member but would like to test the facilities first.

Remember, any time you ask for things, do it with dignity and respect for yourself and the other person. If you beg or show no respect for yourself, you will never look like you belong among the elite. And if you are arrogant or show no respect to the staff, you will come across as impertinent and ill-mannered.

Be elegant, always!

OPERA, THEATRE, BALLET

Affluent people are lovers and supporters of performing arts and attend performances regularly. So, find all the theatres and opera houses in your city and make a habit of going. Trust me; it will enrich your life!

Even for those of you who don't want to meet affluent people, performing arts should be part of your life!

COUNTRY CLUBS / GOLF CLUBS / TENNIS CLUBS / SAILING CLUBS / POLO CLUBS / HORSE RACING CLUBS
CAR RACING CLUBS / SKI CLUBS / ROWING CLUBS

Wealthy people often socialise and play sports at these prestigious establishments. Although you must be a member to attend, when you have a network of influential individuals, there is always someone who knows someone who is a member of such clubs.

There are ways to get invited, probably not immediately, but later, as you gain people's trust.

When you get invited, read the rules beforehand to ensure you are appropriately attired and enjoy the vibe and the people. It makes a beautiful day out and a great way to network.

~ 60 ~

HOW TO MOVE TO AN AFFLUENT AREA ON A BUDGET

I'll share with you three methods which have proved successful:

1st Method

In the well-to-do areas, some period buildings with five or six floors don't have lifts. Probably because they once belonged to affluent families who used the higher floors for servants. When those buildings were converted into apartments, there was no room to install a lift. And without a lift, the upper floors are not desirable to the current market.

Most people don't want to go through the inconvenience of climbing five-six flights of stairs every time they come home, so they don't have a problem paying more money to live on a lower floor, or in a building with a working lift.

Therefore, the landlords rent the top-floor places (in buildings without lifts) for much less than a flat of the same size on a lower floor.

On many occasions, in the landlord's attempt to make them appealing to potential tenants, the top-floor places are newly refurbished. As a result, you may find a beautiful little apartment on the fifth or sixth floor in an affluent area for a fraction of the price. And you can turn the lack of lift to your advantage:

- Stair climbing will keep you fit.
- You don't have to carry many shopping bags since you don't have a huge family.
- You'll buy your groceries in smaller quantities more often, keeping your food as fresh as possible.
- You will live in an excellent neighbourhood, surrounded by rich people, making it easier to build a network of wealthy individuals and, possibly, meet a partner.

Visit all the estate agents in all the affluent areas, tell them what you are after and leave your details, so they can contact you if any places on the top floors of buildings without a lift become available. You can tell them you want to live in the area but have a limited budget. If you are honest with them about having a limited budget, the agents will not waste your time showing you places that are too pricey for you. You must be clear about what you want. Efficiency is key to a successful outcome.

2nd Method

Read carefully and follow these steps:
- Put leaflets through letterboxes in affluent neighbourhoods, stating that you are looking for a room to rent.
- Mention that you are a professional working in a corporation (or whatever your line of work is) and that you can provide work and character references.
- Leave your name, number and email address. By mentioning these things, you look trustworthy even before people meet you. An example of the text you can write:

"Dear Residents,

My name is Jane Jennison; I work as a bookkeeper for "BrunLevent&Co" and am looking to rent a room in your neighbourhood. I have work and

character references and all the relevant paperwork.

If you know someone interested in taking in a lodger, please pass on my details: 0770 777 7777, jane.jenninson@google.com.

Many thanks and have a beautiful day!"

- The leaflets should be on an unfolded A4 paper, written in bold capital letters in the largest font that allows you to fit everything on one page.
- Don't write too much text, or it will not be read.
- The writing should be large enough to be illegible even if the person doesn't bend to pick up the paper.
- Put only one A4 sheet through each door, even if it's clear that there are multiple flats in that building.

Remember to be considerate and leave only one leaflet for each entrance! One piece of paper will not be seen as junk mail. Multiple pieces of paper may infuriate the people who live there.

a) If the paper falls with the writing up (when pushed through the letterbox), the letters are large enough for anyone entering the building to read, even without picking it up from the floor.

- If your announcement is not of interest to them, they will ignore it.
- If they have an available room and want to rent it, they'll contact you.

b) If the paper falls with the writing down, someone entering the building may be curious to know if it's an important announcement, so they pick it up.

- If the ad is not of interest to them, they will put it with the rest of the mail for the other neighbours.
- If they are interested, they'll get in touch.

A person may live in a house/flat with spare rooms, but it doesn't necessarily occur to them to take in a lodger. However, by seeing the advert written in a polite and articulate tone, they may want to meet you.

And sometimes, the decision to take in a lodger may not even be for the money:
- It could be because they travel often and want to know that the place is looked after, in their absence.
- They may have a pet and hope to find someone to look after it while they are away.

- There may be an elderly person who has plenty of available space and would like to share it with someone who can be there in case of emergency.

- There may be many reasons why a person with the extra room may consider taking in a lodger, after seeing your ad and deciding that you are trustworthy.

By dropping the announcement through the letterbox, you are implanting the idea in someone's head, as they may start seeing the benefits of sharing their place. It's called creating opportunities for yourself!

Stay safe, and when you meet the person for the first time, do it in a public place, tell a friend where you'll be, or go accompanied.

3rd Method

If by now you've made some new wealthy friends, tell them about your plans to move and ask them to let you know if they hear of anyone who has a place to rent or looking for a lodger.

Without putting yourself down or making yourself look pitiful, you can mention that you are looking for something modest, so they know not to show you something extravagant.

Tell them that you want to make some changes in your life and would like to live closer to work, the cultural areas, the city centre, etc.

As usual, someone will know someone who knows someone who may have something available. Always ask!

***

Now that you know three successful methods, try them simultaneously, so you can increase your odds and find reasonably priced places in an affluent area.

You may find something fast. Or it may take some time. But if you are consistent and do it right, you WILL find something!

Living in an affluent area will change your life. Therefore, giving up is not an option! Instead, put in the work, and eventually, you will get results!

***

After finding the place and moving to your desired area, learn the neighbourhood. You may even know the neighbourhood if you explored it before.

All the wealthy areas have wine stores which do wine-tasting evenings for the locals. So go to each of them and leave your business cards, so they can call you if they organise events.

Do the same with local art galleries. Numerous art galleries have openings with a reception or an informal party when they launch a new artist, so leave your business card and ask them to invite you.

When you attend a gallery opening event, be considered and well mannered:
- Don't touch the art.
- Don't take flash photography.
- Read a little about the artist after you get the invitation and before coming to the event.
- Don't drink too much.
- Take an interest in the art.

Attending a gallery opening is a free lesson in art and an excellent opportunity to learn something new. The artists are fascinating; they all have compelling stories and unique styles of expressing themselves through art. Learn about them!

And, of course, besides expanding your sphere of interest and knowledge, a local gallery opening is an opportunity to meet local people who can help you build your social network.

Explore all the places in your new neighbourhood. Get information on future events from local libraries, town halls and by signing up for newsletters from local businesses, art and culture places, and churches (for concerts and other cultural events).

If moving is not an option just yet, you must spend all your spare time in affluent areas. Follow the same steps to find ways to get invited to local events and make time to attend as many as you can, even if you must travel.

The sooner you expand your network, the faster you encounter opportunities that will change your life.

~ 61 ~

SKILLS TO LEARN

Apart from the social skills, which, if you studied the book thoroughly, you should master by now, it is helpful to know a few other things which may come in handy.

Swimming
If you don't know how to swim, it's wise to learn, as it is likely that you will be invited to pool and yacht parties. You don't have to swim like an Olympian, but knowing basic swimming would boost your confidence, and it's an excellent skill to possess, as you never know when you may need it.

Horse riding
Many affluent people are interested in horses or equestrian sports, and should you ever be invited to go horse riding, it would be good to know that you can stay on a horse.

Skiing
The rich like to holiday in fabulous ski resorts, and being out on the slopes during the day and socialising in a cosy chalet in the evening can be magical! Take some private skiing lessons before you go on holiday, so you cover the basics. You can find indoor snow centres in many large cities. Research where they are and save up for some private lessons.

Tennis
Belonging to a tennis club is not uncommon among the elite, and many people in high society circles enjoy the perks of some of

the most exclusive sports clubs with great tennis courts. So, take up tennis, and you will be invited to play and socialise.

Ballroom dancing
Nowadays, there are only a few places where one can use their dancing abilities, so you shouldn't prioritise it, but consider taking lessons at some point. Moreover, dancing has excellent health benefits and can improve posture and deportment. And you will make a great impression if you can waltz or tango gracefully at a gala event.

Playing an instrument
This is an impressive skill, and it teaches you self-discipline and improves mental performance and focus, among other benefits. But if you decide to learn to play an instrument, do it for yourself and don't impose your "Chopsticks" or a mediocre rendition of "Fur Elise" on others. Most people in high society are exposed to the best music and musicians, and you will make everyone feel awkward if you start showing your beginner's skills on a grand piano at a gathering. So, be considerate. Don't start playing the instrument at a gathering unless you are at an advanced level and are invited to play!

***

So, regarding skills to learn, cover first swimming, horse riding, skiing and tennis. And you can leave the ballroom dancing and playing an instrument for later.

Paying for private lessons to learn the skills above can be expensive, but they will be worth the investment in the long term. Research and find vouchers and special deals to reduce costs and learn the basics. You will improve with time and by practising.

~ 62 ~

YOUR SOCIAL MEDIA

Social platforms are widely used and have become the primary sources of information about a person. The habit of checking updates is so ingrained in people's minds that it's the first thing they do in the morning and the last thing they do at night.

So, if someone wants to find out more about a person, they will go on their social platforms and do a bit of "stalking":
- Employers do it to understand what a job candidate does in their free time.

- New acquaintances do it to learn more about a person they just met.
- And even potential lovers do it out of curiosity.

To be truly elegant is essential to keep your social platforms classy:

- If, in real life, you don't sit down with all your 600 "virtual friends" to show them your bikini pictures, it's unnecessary to upload them on your Facebook and Instagram. Instead, a few tasteful snaps of you wearing clothes are more than enough.

- Bad grammar is another way to spoil your image. So, if you don't master the grammar, be sure to check, double check and triple-check before posting something on social media.

- Don't rant! If you found a bug in your salad, you don't agree with the current mayor, or the rubbish wasn't collected on time, don't feel compelled to write on Facebook. You will get better results if you direct your complaint to the source.

- Don't be a troll and disagree with everyone, getting into arguments.

That shows frustration and lack of manners.

- Don't share tragic stories of animals or children whenever you read one. While people should be aware of certain things, too much negative information harms you and those reading your feeds.

- Don't overwhelm your followers with your religious, spiritual, or political views. When you reach a level of spirituality where you feel content, you don't need to convert everyone to your new way of life. The same goes for politics.

- Not all the material things you buy or every place you visit must end up on your social media. Be discreet about what you do with your everyday life. Not all of it should be shared on social media.

If you are an avid user of social media platforms, do it with wisdom and class and don't get lost in the virtual space. You will be judged by what you post.

63

FIRST DATE

You completed the entire journey of elevating yourself; you now have a great network of friends and acquaintances, and someone you like asked you out.

What do you do on your first date?

If he suggested a restaurant and the place is new to you, go on their website and check out the menu to have an idea of the dishes they serve. It's much more elegant to order within a few minutes of opening the menu than to keep the waiter for a long time standing next to you until you ask about every dish.

If the first date happens in your city, try not to come by public transport. Instead, take a taxi if you can. Public transport can make you flustered and anxious, especially if it's hot or during rush hour. Take a taxi, and leave home early, so you can arrive on time and be composed and serene.

Ideally, when you arrive at the restaurant, you would visit the lavatory before being shown to the table, to see if you look impeccable. It's easier to do this in certain restaurants, depending on their size and layout. In smaller restaurants, visiting the lavatory may be slightly tricky without your date noticing you coming in. If you cannot get to the lavatory for a final look-over, do it in the taxi just before you arrive. So, check your makeup, nose, teeth, breath, hair, and outfit and ensure everything is tidy and fresh.

When you are escorted to the table, the waiter brings you the menu; you take it, thank them, and scan it. Just because you informed yourself from their website, it doesn't mean you should now order without even opening the menu at the table. Sometimes, they may change the dishes and not update the website. You must also wait patiently for the waiter to tell you the specials before you order. Then, you thank them again.

Now that your table manners are excellent, you are confident and elegant while eating:
- You open the napkin or sit back while the waiter does it for you (depending on the restaurant's policy).
- Your bread plate is on the left.
- Your water glass is on the right.
- You hold the wine/champagne glass by its stem.

- You use your cutlery from the outside to the inside.
- Your index fingers are flat on the knife and the fork; you never wave them in the air while you talk and never hold them both in one hand.
- You rest the cutlery at 3:40 when you take a break from eating.
- When you finish, place them at 6:30 (or 4:20 or 3:15).
- You thank the restaurant staff whenever they bring something or fill your glass.
- Your back is always straight, and your elbows are never on the table.
- You are graceful and relaxed, and you never, under any circumstances, comment on his table manners if you think they are not impeccable. Good manners and elegance are about making people feel good in your company. Otherwise, you'd be just a snob.

By now, you are also mastering the art of small talk, so you know how to avoid controversial topics and subjects which may result in disagreements. Therefore, religion, money and politics are not to be discussed.

Don't ask him if he has Facebook, Instagram, Snapchat, or any social platforms. Many rich people don't have time for social platforms, or if they use some, they are very private and only share their social media with family and close friends. So, he may find your question childish and indiscreet, and there may not be a second date.

Don't ask him what he does for a living or how much money he makes. Knowing his wealth shouldn't be of interest to you anyway.

If you met him in the right circumstances, the fact that he's wealthy is implied. If you are curious about his field of activity, you can ask him that, as long as you don't go into specific details and try to find out things that he may not be willing to share with you.

Let it be a conversation where you share a little about yourself too, not just ask questions. Also, remember to share, but not to overshare! Don't talk badly about your former relationships, don't be too graphic or explicit about anything, and don't shock him with things about your liberal family or friends.

The first date should be light-hearted and breezy. Making each other laugh and enjoying a nice meal is all you can expect from a first date. Don't drink too much and don't spend the night together, as it will look desperate. Have fun but remain classy and composed!

An elegant woman who exudes femininity, charisma, confidence, and humour will intrigue any man. And he will want to know more.

NOTES:
- Check out the location and the menu of the restaurant.
- Be elegant and tastefully dressed.
- Come by taxi.
- Have a final check before meeting your date.
- Remember your table manners.
- Stand and sit straight and confident.
- Keep the small talk light and pleasant.
- Don't be indiscreet, and don't overshare.
- Be polite to the restaurant staff.
- Don't get drunk.
- Don't end up going home with your date.
- Remain elegant, feminine and charismatic.

64

THE UNNECESSARY GAMES

Some women play unnecessary games. For example, just because she has heard or read somewhere that "you shouldn't give the impression that you sit around waiting for his call", a woman playing games will take it as "a dating rule" and avoid answering his call, pretending she's busy. That's an unnecessary game.

If you are busy, it's understandable. But if you are not busy, answer the phone. You are not a teenager!

A dignified woman doesn't play games and wouldn't like the guy to reciprocate in the same way. So, it's time to ditch the tests you've learned from friends and gossip magazines and start behaving like a lady.

If he calls and you can take the call, then take the call! He may only have a little time and wanted to thank you for a lovely evening and invite you out again. Be polite, check your schedule and be honest! If you cannot make it when he's next available, tell him. But if you can make it, then go and see him!

Those meetings at the beginning of a relationship are essential in finding out about each other and seeing if you have things in common and share similar interests.

If you disapprove of his ideas and lifestyle, it's better to know at the beginning. Not approving of his way of being and making compromises will result in resentment later.

If you don't like how he is, don't embark on a relationship hoping he will change for you. If you start with that mentality, the relationship is already doomed.

Remember that, although the book is about meeting high-calibre people, the goal is finding a man with whom you can connect and fall in love. It teaches you about the changes you need to make so you can raise the standards for yourself and the people with whom you want to surround yourself. Don't settle for a man who is not a gentleman just because he is rich. By agreeing to do that, you go against your principles.

Be only with a man who has a gentle nature and treats you well. There are many such men; it is up to you to find them.

But it's essential to elevate yourself first. If you are loud and obnoxious, the men who will notice you will be the ones who may be looking for a bit of fun, not the authentic gentlemen.

The genuinely lovely guys will want to be far away from women who misbehave. So, if you attract lousy men, it's because you may be doing something wrong.

Raise your standards, elevate yourself physically, mentally and intellectually, and behave like a lady. Then, you will attract men with high standards.

Ignore the misconception that behaving like a lady is old-fashioned and boring. On the contrary, acting like a lady means that you have impeccable manners while still exuding femininity, which is a timeless trait. Femininity is one of the essential characteristics in this process, because most affluent men are high achievers, alpha males in a dog-eat-dog world, and they admire the elegance and the gentleness of a woman who enjoys being a woman.

And no, it doesn't mean that rich men prefer women who are pretty but not smart! On the contrary, rich men are besotted with intelligent women who are also feminine. What rich men don't necessarily like would be an intelligent woman who behaves like a man.

It's nothing wrong with being a masculine woman if that is your personality and you are not interested in finding a wealthy gentleman. There is someone for everyone.

The book is about women wanting to date the kind of men who are high achievers and want someone gentle and more feminine by their side to balance their masculinity. Therefore, generally, rich men are not attracted to macho women. So, if you are masculine and want to embark on this journey, you must soften your way of being.

On the other extreme is being too salacious. Gentlemen don't like women who exaggerate with their seductive and flirtatious behaviour. That side of you should be intimate, and you shouldn't display it publicly and with everyone.

It's OK to have sex appeal. But sex appeal should come from how you look after your general appearance, from your body language and from the experience lived in that moment when you exude sex appeal.

So, for example, if you are attending a funeral or other sombre occasion, you shouldn't be the "main attraction" because your lasciviousness is too hard to ignore. That is not sex appeal. It is being overly sexual at an inappropriate time.

Suppose you are on a date with a guy. If you like and enjoy each other's company, you will automatically start flirting, and it will not feel inappropriate or forced. It will be natural.

But flirting shamelessly with any guy you meet could be interpreted as desperate, or you could be branded as promiscuous or a woman of easy virtue. You shouldn't flirt with someone without knowing if the guy is single and if you like him beyond his looks. Yes, he may show interest in you, but it would be for the wrong reasons: he may be married and looking for a little fun or single and looking for the same thing. And that is precisely the opposite of the man you want to attract.

Being charming is different from being flirtatious. **You can be lovely towards everyone you meet, but it is not advisable**

to be flirtatious with everyone you meet. Flirt happens after you get to know the man who brings out your playful side. A man needs to work a little to discover that side of you. If he sees it too early, he will not think he is special. He will believe it's in your nature to seduce every man you meet. And a man with high standards will be put off by this behaviour.

In conclusion, being a lady differentiates you from a sexual prowess and makes you feminine and elegant.

However, if you are happy being flirtatious, or tough and masculine, and you are not interested in finding a gentleman, ignore this book and enjoy your life! Don't get outraged by something that doesn't interest you!

~ 65 ~

AND THEN, WHAT?

Assuming the first date and the dates after went well, you are now with a high-value man. Enjoy your relationship and the new you, but don't stagnate! Instead, continue to learn, improve, and educate yourself!

When you started your transformation, you embarked on a journey which made you experience a different life. You've raised your standards, and looking back at your old life, you see how far you've come.

If things go well and you are both happy, this man may be the one, which would be a happy ending. However, if the relationship doesn't last, you must be prepared to maintain your new standards with **your** resources.

So, learn how to make money. Don't feel guilty about wanting more for yourself, and it's no shame in asking for help from the man in your life, as long as you do it with dignity and consideration.

How would you ask for help?
Tell him about your goals and aspirations and ask for guidance and help.

- Maybe you always wanted a degree and were worried you couldn't afford it. Discuss with him; he may want to help you with your studies.

- You may want to start a business and have the concept but don't know how to go about it. Ask the man in your life to help with advice; if he likes your business idea, he may even invest in it. Or he may connect you with people in that field.

- Or perhaps you have a hidden talent but never felt comfortable showing your creations. Now it's time to build that website, organise a good marketing campaign and display your artwork for people to see. In the elite circle, there is always someone who knows someone who can help you in any field. So, ask that favour and he will introduce you to people.

- You may like cooking, and you've always dreamed of having your YouTube cooking channel. He has a state-of-the-art kitchen which he never uses. Put it to use and start your little business.

Talk to him about your goals and aspirations: studying, opening a business, or doing something that requires guidance and financial backing. You may find that he would be delighted to help you achieve your dream. If you managed to conquer this man's interest and heart, your ambitions and aspirations would be just as captivating to him, as he undoubtedly sees you as an intelligent and driven woman, and he is proud of you.

If you don't have a dream, start thinking of one! Because no matter how much you like to be spoiled and looked after, financial independence feels a million times better!

- ✓ **You worked hard to make changes and to discipline yourself to get here.**
- ✓ **You built an excellent network of wealthy friends and acquaintances.**
- ✓ **You even "bagged" your millionaire.**
- ✓ **You reached that goal.**
- ✓ **You are unstoppable!**
- ✓ **So, continue progressing, and learn to make money and build wealth.**
- ✓ **Set a new goal.**
- ✓ **Find a career dream you want to accomplish and continue your transformation from the refined woman you've become into a successful professional, an entrepreneur or anything you want to achieve.**
- ✓ **Never stagnate!**
- ✓ **Always progress!**

Dr Spencer Johnson wrote a simple book on dealing with changes and adapting to something new.

The book is "Who Moved My Cheese?"

The story is about **two mice** and **two little people** who were feeding themselves from the same "cheese station". They had the same daily routine: wake up and go to the cheese station to feed themselves. One morning, they found that there was no more cheese.

The mice possessed survival instincts, so when they were faced with the lack of cheese, they immediately started searching for a new place to feed themselves. And when they found a new "cheese station", while feeding themselves from it, they inspected it daily to see how it was reducing, to ensure they would not be surprised when the cheese finishes again.

The little people possessed superior intelligence, so when faced with the lack of cheese, they started wondering who moved their cheese and why it happened to them. They wasted time and energy getting angry and frustrated, instead of focusing on what to do to feed themselves. Due to their fear of the unknown, they didn't venture into the maze immediately (like the mice) to find another cheese station. They thought it was "too scary out there". Instead, they moaned, complained, and wished things would return to how they were. It was nice and comfortable before, and now everything is scary and uncertain. So, because of their moaning and complaining, it took them much longer to get into the mindset of leaving their comfort zone and finding another "cheese station".

Changes will always occur in life, whether you are ready or not. But you shouldn't fear changes. Instead, adapt to changes, because staying in your comfort zone and not facing challenges is not productive and will not help you grow.

So, just like the little mice, when change happens, adapt as soon as possible, and look for new opportunities. Don't waste time like the little people moaning, complaining, and blaming others for your situation.

BE KIND!

If you paid attention to all the chapters, you should now be kinder to yourself:
- Kind to yourself through how you eat, drink, exercise and perform your beauty routine.
- Kind to yourself by healing past traumas.
- Kind to yourself by paying attention to your thoughts and your internal voice.
- Kind to yourself by practising gratitude.
- Kind to yourself by removing yourself from harmful people and situations.
- Kind to yourself by feeding your soul with nature, culture and beautiful things.

And because you learned to be kind to yourself, you will automatically practice kindness towards others:
- Kind to animals. If you can't have a pet is understandable. But if you are unkind to animals is unacceptable!
- Kind to the environment by being more thoughtful about what you buy

and helping the planet in any way possible: from recycling to planting a tree or helping environmental campaigns.

- Kind to everyone you meet: from the people in the most modest positions to those of the highest rank. You are not elegant if you show respect to a wealthy person, but you are unkind to the toilet attendant.
- Kind to those of a different background, race, nationality, sexual orientation, or social status.
- Kind to people who don't share your views. You can have different opinions, but you mustn't be disrespectful.
- Kind to people who don't have good manners. Remember that having good manners is about making people feel comfortable around you. Pointing out people's mistakes is neither elegant nor kind. If someone asks you to teach them, do it, but don't humiliate them.
- Kind to people who want to do things differently from you. Everyone is allowed to express themselves in different ways: it may be a particular kind of fashion style, a genre of music, another way of life etc. Be kind to them even if you

disapprove of what they like. As long as they don't hurt someone and it's not illegal or immoral, they have the right to do as they wish.

- Kind to people who don't approve of your lifestyle, changes or the new you. Be kind to these people because not everyone understands that, as long as one doesn't hurt others and it's not immoral or illegal, one has the right to do as one wishes. But you understand it, and you are kind to them too.

Be kind in any way you can think of, and more!

~ 67 ~

BELIEVE

You must believe! And I know that if you are reading this book now while sitting on a platform waiting for the train to take you to a job that you hate, you have very little money in your account, your relationships until now have been insignificant, your life lacks excitement, you have mediocre friendships, you don't think that you are in great shape, you may think that the dream of meeting a millionaire is quite far-fetched.

The book didn't reveal a magic way to make it happen. It just enumerated a bunch of things you must change in your life. And you may even start doing some of the things mentioned in the book, but you don't feel fully committed because you don't quite believe this can be done.

Well, start believing! Believe with every single fibre of your being! Be deeply devoted to your goal!

Your current situation is the result of the decisions you made in the past. If you want different circumstances in future, start making different decisions **now**! Repeating the same things will not yield different results.

If you did it your way and are unsatisfied, try it this way, and you may be surprised. But you must follow the book chapter by chapter, like a manual. Don't skip anything!

The book is titled "How To Bag A Millionaire", but it's not about finding a wealthy man to use for your material needs. It's about raising your standards to start networking in different circles, and you will meet many millionaires, make new friends, and acquaintances and possibly even meet the man of your dreams. By raising your standards, you will begin to live a different life: a more elegant and content life. You will understand how important it is to look after every aspect of your health: mental and physical. You will learn to have kinder thoughts towards yourself and others. You will learn to quiet your mind, value your time, and avoid toxic people and situations. You will learn to keep things simple and organise your life better.

Using the law of attraction only works if you believe in your goals strongly enough to take the first step and have the grit to carry on:

- Form your thoughts.
- Start feeling how it is to have what you desire.
- **TAKE ACTION AND WORK TOWARDS YOUR GOALS!**
- Enjoy the results.

Sometimes you'll see the results immediately; other times, it will take longer. And in some cases, the results don't necessarily show in the form you initially wanted. But if your belief is strong, if you take action and work towards your dreams, the results will show in an even better form.

Throughout history, all the successful people applied the law of attraction but didn't have a name for it. If you ask every single one, they'll tell you the same story:
- First, the dream started as a thought: "how would it be if ..."
- Then, they lived and felt their dream with all their senses, even when some said it could not be done.
- And the most crucial part is that they took action and never stopped until they achieved that dream.

The success didn't just come to them. The grit made them succeed, the staying power that drove them through failures and moments when they wanted to give up.

Believing that they will accomplish the proposed goal was their driving force. They believed in their dream, saw, tasted, felt, and smelled their vision and took actions - continuously, without giving up.

You must do the same! It can be a long process. It can be a lonely and tiring process, so brace yourself and be prepared to go through all the obstacles coming your way!

Feeding yourself well, getting enough rest, and keeping your spirits high are crucial factors, not only for your physical health but for your mental one too. So don't skip ahead; follow each step and believe in your dream, even in your lowest moments.

Hang on in there, and you will grow! And with growth comes satisfaction. When you see progress, you will not want to go back. Instead, you will want to go forward because looking back will seem so far away, and the improvements will be evident, and you know that it can only get better.

You have the right to live a healthy and abundant life, be in a happy relationship and enjoy a successful career. So go and claim that right!

Your journey starts now, with the first step. Take that step!

Made in United States
Troutdale, OR
12/19/2023

16121708R00201